MILLENNIUM S
OF
WARRINGTON

R. Waywell.

God giveth the increase.

present
from
DOT.
12-2-2001

Warrington Archaeological and Historical Society

Cover: Warrington Market Place in 1834, taken from Baine's 'Lancashire', with permission from Warrington Borough Council, Libraries and Information Services.

Typeset and design: Jen Darling of *Alfresco Books*

Production: MFP Design & Print

FOREWORD

This book was never intended to be a rewrite of the history of Warrington, which has been adequately covered before. We have been seeking to find from within the town some interesting and possibly entertaining snippets of life as it was in times past — a scrapbook of memories to celebrate the new Millennium.

It was obvious that the Society's modest financial resources would be inadequate to cover all the publication costs. However, following a suggestion from Mr John Heald, one of our auditors, we approached *The Millennium Festival Awards for All* committee and I am pleased to acknowledge here their grant of £2,200 towards the cost of this project. Their generous support is much appreciated and has allowed us to go ahead with confidence.

Thanks must also go to Eric Naylor and Ray Hunt, who have borne the brunt of the work leading up to publication.

Finally, may I commend our *Millennium Scrapbook of Warrington* to all who have an interest in the town and the rich tapestry of its history. I hope you will find as much pleasure in reading the book as we have found in putting it together.

J K Ashworth, Chairman

PREFACE

In the wake of several enquiries to me, as the then Secretary of the *Warrington Archaeological and Historical Society*, asking if we had anything planned to mark the Millennium, and having to reply, "nothing as yet," gave me the idea that the Society might publish a book containing contributions from members concerning Warrington's colourful past.

With the approval of the Chairman, the idea was put to a full meeting of the Society and, after open discussion, there was enthusiastic support from members for such a project. Accordingly, at the next executive committee meeting the project was discussed in detail and members were then asked to put forward suitable material for inclusion in a book celebrating the Millennium.

I am grateful to the Chairman, Mr Ken Ashworth, the Vice-Chairman, Mr Ray Hunt, and Mr Harry Wells, with his experience of book publishing, all of whom assisted me with the editing and preparation of the articles. I also appreciate the efforts of our contributors and thank them for their work, supplied at no cost to the Society. The help of the Warrington Museum Services, who supplied several photographs, is also acknowledged with thanks.

Eric J Naylor

CONTENTS

WARRINGTON'S INFAMOUS LORD OF THE MANOR

Eric J Naylor

The infamous Lord of the Manor was no Warringtonian. After 400 years in the hands of the Botelers, the Manor passed to Robert Dudley, the 14th Earl of Leicester. It came to him from Edward Boteler, literally the last of the Botelers, for Edward, who died in 1586, left no issue despite having been married twice. His first wife was Jane, daughter of Richard Brooke of Norton, and the second was Margaret Maisterson of Nantwich, whose grandfather was Sir Thomas Grosvenor of Eaton.

Despite being well connected, Edward was somewhat of a rakish, dissolute character, who squandered his patrimony and had to settle his estates on the Earl of Leicester some years before his death. Little is known of Leicester's occupancy of the manor house — Bewsey Old Hall — but more is known of his place in English history.

Bewsey Old Hall

The Earl of Leicester was well connected and had a very colourful and distinguished life as courtier and politician, despite some infamous episodes. He was born in 1532, the 5th son of John Dudley, the 19th Earl of Warwick and 1st Duke of Northumberland. In his early life as Lord Dudley, well before his days in Warrington, his first transgression was in joining in the attempt to set Lady Jane Grey on the throne of England. For this he was tried for high treason and condemned to death. However, then as now, it is not what you know but who you know that counts, and he obtained his pardon and was set free.

At that time he was a Roman Catholic, but after Elizabeth gained the throne he became a zealous Protestant and soon found favour in the Queen's eyes. His first appointment by her was as Master of the Horse, then in 1559 he was installed a Knight of the Garter. He received so many important posts and favours from the Queen that it was generally supposed that she entertained ideas of marrying him. This raised the rather indelicate question: "Was she the 'virgin queen' as reputed?"

Lord Robert Dudley had, however, married Amy Robsart in 1550 and her accidental and sudden death in 1560 caused scandalous tongues to wag. Amy died at Cumnor Place, an old manor house in Cumnor, about three miles west of Oxford. She was said to have fallen down a flight of stairs and broken her neck. An old book of mine has a chapter entitled 'Cumnor Hall and the Fate of Amy Robsart'.

She was apparently staying at Dudley's request as a guest of the owner, one Anthony Forster, who has a favourable epitaph in Cumnor Church, but who in Ashmole's *Antiquities of Berkshire* is represented as one of the parties to the 'murder' of Amy Dudley. Ashmole was only born in 1617 so he must have been writing very much in retrospect, but it serves to emphasise what a long-lasting scandal Amy's death must have been.

An inquest was held, and Milton Waldman, in his book *Elizabeth and Leicester,* refers at length to the inquest in his chapter 'Murder,

Accident or Suicide', to which the reader is referred. No-one could be found who had seen Lady Dudley fall; she was just found dead at the bottom of the stairs, and so the question, 'Did she fall or was she pushed?' was never answered and the jury returned a verdict of accidental death.

There was a general impression that the death was suspicious and the conclusion reached later was that, although Dudley was innocent of direct participation in the crime, the unhappy lady was sacrificed to his ambition and was murdered by persons who hoped to profit by Dudley's elevation to Consort of the Queen.

This episode behind him, the Queen's continuing affection was shown in the grant of Kenilworth Castle and Manor in 1563, and by his creation as Earl of Leicester in 1564. Then, when Elizabeth came to realise that marriage to him was politically impossible, she tried to persuade him to marry the widowed Mary Queen of Scots!

Leicester's place at Court was repeatedly put in jeopardy by his flirtations, particularly when, in 1573, he took as his second wife the widow of Lord Sheffield and daughter of Lord William Howard of Effingham. She bore him a son in 1573 who was christened Robert after his father. In 1578 he also married Lettice Knollys, the widowed Countess of Essex. His former marriage to Lady Sheffield, who was still living, had been solemnised secretly and he tried to deny it. Lady Sheffield always maintained that they were legally married but was frightened into secrecy by Leicester's threat that he would poison her. Whether young Robert was legitimate or not does not seem to have been resolved, but his father's conduct was another of his infamies.

Other events earning Leicester the description of 'the infamous Lord of the Manor' relate to his suspected activities as a poisoner. There were so many people who died conveniently for Leicester that it was hard to believe he was not involved in their deaths. Sir Nicholas Throgmorton, dining at Leicester's house, was one, and his first wife, Amy, of course was another.

The Earl of Essex, too, sent to Ireland on the Queen's service (thought to be by Leicester's influence), died suddenly in Dublin and poison was suspected. It was common knowledge that Leicester and Essex's wife Lettice had been having an affair for some time. After Essex's death Leicester married Lettice, as mentioned before, and they had one son who died at the early age of four, 'the noble impe' as he was described on his tomb in Beauchamp Chapel, Warwick. Cause of death is unknown, although Waldman in his book *Elizabeth and Leicester* says that his enemies later found that poison was administered by a nurse, at his father's instigation as he was a hunch-back.

In 1584 a book appeared in Antwerp which was later called *Leycester's Commonwealth*. It listed his public crimes and catalogued his more domestic misdeeds. In vain did Queen Elizabeth by an Order in Council attempt to forbid its circulation, which shows what an impression the book made upon the public. His nephew, Sir Philip Sidney, also leaped to his uncle's defence, but with no more success than Elizabeth. The publication succeeded in turning Leicester into a legendary monster.

Leicester tried to regain his lost reputation and power, leaving England for the Low Countries in June 1587, then returning when England was expecting the Spanish Armada. And in July 1588, Elizabeth, still infatuated with him, appointed him Lieutenant-General of all the forces assembled at Tilbury to resist the threatened invasion. This never came, for the Armada was defeated in August.

Leicester remained in London for the great rejoicings, then left on holiday. He meant to visit Buxton to take the waters, travelling by way of Kenilworth. He wrote to the Queen from Maidenhead and Rycott, the home of Sir John Norris's parents where they had in the past spent pleasant days together. The Queen marked this 'his last letter' and put it in her bedside chest to be re-read. Leicester's holiday journey did not get further than Cornbury Hall near Oxford, for there he died on 4th September 1588. His sudden death was attributed to poison and it was said that he was 'hoist with his own petard'.

He was buried in the Lady Chapel of the Collegiate Chapel at Warwick, where the 'noble impe' already lay, and to his memory was erected a monument with his effigy in armour lying on its back, his Earl's coronet on his head and an effigy of Lettice beside him. The Privy Council must have believed that his death was not natural, for they minutely investigated a report that he had been poisoned by a son of Sir James Crofts in revenge for the imprisonment of his father; but the matter was suddenly dropped.

So ended Warrington's Infamous Lord of the Manor and we are reminded of him only by the names given to new streets as Warrington expanded — Leicester Street and Elizabeth Street (coincidentally very close together) and Dudley Street on the other side of town.

Bibliography

Annals of the Lords of Warrington and Bewsey
by William Beamont

Abbeys, Castles and Ancient Halls of England and Wales
by Timbs and Gunn

Elizabeth and Leicester
by Milton Waldman

ELIAS ASHMOLE (1617- 1692)

J K Ashworth

Elias Ashmole was born in Lichfield in May 1617, into a good yeoman family of that city. His grandfather, Thomas Ashmole, was a master saddler, which was a valued and respected occupation in the days when horse transport was the principle means of travel. At various times he also served as Sheriff, Junior and Senior Bailiff and Justice of the Peace and these services led him to be acknowledged as an established 'gentleman' of Lichfield.

Elias' father was also a saddler but spent many years soldiering, mainly in Ireland. His mother was the daughter of an old, notable and respected Staffordshire family. One of her sisters was the wife of Dr Charles Twisden, Chancellor of the Lichfield diocese. Another sister was the second wife of James Pugit, a Puisne (junior) Baron of the Exchequer in London.

Bearing in mind the normal standards of the 17th century Elias received a good education. He attended Lichfield Grammar School until he was 16 and was a chorister at the Cathedral. Then to further Elias' education, James Pugit took him to London and, together with his two Pugit cousins, he trained in law at Pugit's chambers. By the time he was 21 Elias' diary noted that he had begun to 'solicit in Chancery' and had an 'indifferently good' practice, eventually moving to the Middle Temple.

In the society of the Pugits and their friends he met Eleanor Mainwaring, who was 14 years his senior and came from an ancient gentry family of Cheshire. They married on 27th March 1638 and were very happy.

By 1641, at 24 years of age, his practice had improved and he began to 'keep house' (practice from his own chambers). He was admitted to Clements Inn and was sworn in as an attorney at the Court of Common Pleas. The year 1641, however, was a sad one for him. His wife, expecting their first child, went to stay at her parents' home in Smallwood, Cheshire, where, after a short illness, she died. Ashmole was travelling north on the way to Smallwood but unfortunately had made a brief overnight stop in Lichfield when her death occurred. She was buried in the graveyard at Astbury Church.

The Mainwaring family of Cheshire were numerous, with property around Biddulph, Peover, Knutsford and Kermincham. Ashmole's friendship with his in-laws, which had commenced during his courtship of Eleanor, lasted long after her death.

In 1642, when the Civil War broke out, his connection with the courts led him into the King's service as an officer in the Royalist army and he was posted to Oxford as Commander of Ordnance. During this time he broke the secret military code of the Parliamentary army, which proved of valuable assistance to the Royalists. Also, despite active service at Marston Moor and later at Worcester, he found time to attend Brasenose College, where he studied with distinction.

Ashmole was at Worcester on 24th July 1646, when it was the last Royalist garrison city to surrender. According to the terms of surrender he was required to ride out of the city and never again bear arms against the Parliament of England. To meet this, and the second clause of the surrender, which required all Royalist officers to remove themselves at least 20 miles from London, he decided to go to his father-in-law's house in Cheshire. He did, however, eventually return to the capital and busied himself with writing and translation, his main work having been a catalogue of the Order of the Garter and a listing of Coats of Arms.

Following the Restoration, his association with the courts led him to be presented to King Charles II shortly after the King's return on 25th May 1660, when he landed at Dover. Ashmole appears to have made a good impression on the King for within two days he was sent for again and appointed Windsor Herald of the College of Arms. He seems to have been successful in this while continuing to produce numerous literary works, the most renowned being 'The Institution, Laws and Ceremony of The Most Noble Order of the Garter'.

Elias Ashmole also inherited a most important collection of rarities from his friend, John Tradescant. This he enlarged and it became a basic and vital part of his famous benefaction to Oxford University — the Ashmolean Museum. The first public museum in Britain devoted to natural sciences, it is, of course, the institution for which he is principally remembered.

———————

You, the reader, may by now be wondering why a 'snapshot' of a national 17th century person such as Elias Ashmole should be included in this publication. Let me enlighten you ...

We have heard of the Civil War dividing families but in contrast Ashmole, although he remarried, maintained his friendship and connection with his late wife's family, the Mainwarings of Cheshire, visiting them frequently. On one of these visits Ashmole (a recently serving Royalist Army Officer) and Colonel Henry Mainwaring (Eleanor's kinsman and a Parliamentarian officer, who had played a notable part in the Roundhead's taking of Northwich) together planned and arranged a joint venture.

In October 1646, a few months after the battle of Worcester, they made the short journey to **Warrington** for both to be initiated and accepted into a Lodge of Freemasons. The Freemasons were then an ancient and established society but we are told that the meeting at Warrington on 16th October 1646 is the first recorded and documented initiation of anyone into a Lodge under the jurisdiction of the Grand Lodge of England.

Ashmole recorded this occasion in his diary, naming the seven principal members in attendance with the words, 'all seemed to be men of good standing from Warrington and district'. They were ...

Mr Hugh Brewer Mr James Collier
Mr Richard Sankey Mr Henry Littler
Mr John Ellam Mr Richard Ellam
Mr Richard Penket (Penketh)

Elias died in 1692 and was buried in St Mary's Church, Lambeth, where the words on his tombstone in the Howard Chapel read ...

'While *The Ashmolean* endures he will never die.'

The Cock Hotel

This stood down the second entry on the east side of Bridge Street and was demolished about 1908.

It had associations with Freemasonry. The first Lodge after the institution of Grand Lodges, was one warranted by the Ancients or Athol Grand Lodge and opened at the Cock Hotel as Lodge No. 40.

THE FRENCH CONNECTION

Len Jones

It is possibly not a well known fact that Warrington Academy at one time may have employed the notorious French Revolutionary Jean Paul Marat as a teacher of French. He became infamous as one of the dreaded few, along with Robespierre and Danton, during the Reign of Terror (1789-1793) in Paris.

Marat, alias Monsieur le Maitre (or Mara), was born in 1743 in Neuchatel, Switzerland, where he was educated up to the age of 16. He then left home and came to England in about 1769 when he was about 26. He taught for a short time at the Academy and is believed to have left Warrington around 1772.

The following year he published a philosophical essay on the 'Body and Soul of Man' and was also heavily involved in the publication of a seditious book, 'The Chains of Slavery'. These publications give an insight into the mind and thinking of Marat, who could only be described as a radical revolutionary of the highest order.

He is reported as having been living in Oxford in 1776, where it is alleged he robbed the Ashmolean Museum of 'medals', then tried to sell them. He fled to Ireland, where he was apprehended and arrested in Dublin. He was then tried in Oxford, was convicted and sentenced to five years hard labour in the *Hulks* (prison ships) at Woolwich.

After release he went to live in Bristol, where be became a bookseller but got into debt and was committed to the Debtors' Prison. There he remained until his release by the Society for the Relief of Prisoners for Small Debts. (It is noted that the Society member who had personally released him from jail in Bristol, later identified him as a member of the National Assembly in Paris in 1792.)

On his return to France he became actively involved in the Revolution. In September 1789, following the storming of the Bastille on 14th July, he published a newspaper, *The Friend of the People*, which soon became France's most radical journal. He labelled political moderates as traitors and called for popular violence against them.

Marat was a dangerous fanatic to his enemies and he was in tune with the radical mood that led to the fall of the monarchy in August 1792. He also contributed to the atmosphere of violence that led to the mass executions by guillotine of political and aristocratic prisoners, from April 1792.

Elected to the National Assembly in 1792, he urged dictatorial measures to defend the Revolution. He was also the leader of the Paris Jacobin Club, a revolutionary party which vehemently opposed the Girondins — a right wing Republican party of the Revolution originating in the Gironde district of France. The Girondins were overthrown by the Jacobins, who became all powerful, but Marat did not live to see this.

On 13th July 1793 Marat, working in his bath where he regularly treated a skin complaint, was attacked and stabbed to death. His assailant was a young woman from Normandy called Charlotte Corday, a Girondist sympathiser, who held Marat responsible for the Reign of Terror.

She was taken by Marat's friends, condemned to death by a Revolutionary tribunal and guillotined on 17th July 1793. Marat's life was one of a complex personality, with varying manifestations of character and behaviour. His varied life as a teacher, doctor, artist, felon, convict, journalist, politician and terrorist, is intriguing and also, of course, has a Warrington connection.

PRIMROSE LEAGUE

WARRINGTON HABITATION, (No. 1469).

Ruling Councillor - - - - - *MRS. REYNOLDS.*

THE ANNUAL

General Meeting

OF THIS HABITATION WILL BE HELD IN

ASSEMBLY ROOM, CONSERVATIVE CLUB, SANKEY-ST.

On Thursday Evening, May 16, 1895,

At 7-30 o'clock, prompt.

TO BE FOLLOWED BY A —

MEETING OF CONSERVATIVES AND LIBERAL UNIONISTS

At 8 o'clock. The Meeting will be open to all Conservatives and Liberal Unionists
and will be addressed by

ROBERT PIERPOINT, ESQ., M.P.,

ROBERT DAVIES, ESQ., JOHN WHITE, ESQ., J.P., C.C., and other Gentlemen.

A ✤ CONCERT

WILL ALSO BE HELD DURING THE EVENING IN WHICH

MRS. ATKIN, MR. HERBERT BOOTH, MR. J. S. HAYNES, MR. ALFRED
GROUNDS, and the LATCHFORD QUARTETTE PARTY will take part.

Accompanist - - - *MR. PERCY RANDALL.*

ADMISSION FREE to all Conservatives, Liberal Unionists, and their Friends.

Printed by James Wood, 46, Sankey Street, Warrington.

SYLVANUS REYNOLDS (1830-1887)

Eric J Naylor

Sylvanus Reynolds entered into partnership with his uncle at Latchford Tannery, becoming by 1868 the sole owner. By 1878 he was also chairman of three companies: Arthur Waring & Co., also tanners, in Winwick Street; the Castle Rubber Company and the Lion Hotel Company in Bridge Street. He was a trustee of the local Blue Coat School, a Borough Magistrate and one-time member of Warrington Borough Council, being an active and prominent Conservative.

Sylvanus Reynolds was secretary of the Warrington Conservative Association in 1860 and president later, and was involved with the building of the Conservative Club premises in Sankey Street, which opened in 1884. The minutes of the preliminary meeting of the **Primrose League** Warrington Habitation No.1469, held at the Conservative Club on 21st May 1886, under the chairmanship of the Mayor, Joseph Harrison, record that Captain Reynolds was present and was appointed to the Executive Council. To this organisation his widow, Jane, was also appointed Ruling Councillor in 1889.

Sylvanus Reynolds had earlier demonstrated his patriotism by joining the Warrington Volunteers on their formation. In 1862 he was promoted to Captain and continued to be known by this title until his death on 13th November 1887.

His sudden and untimely demise at the age of 57 was a grievous loss to the town and the Conservative party. It occurred the day after a shooting incident in which, whilst climbing a fence, his gun was accidentally discharged, causing extensive injury to a leg which had to be amputated at a nearby house.

His funeral was an impressive occasion, with hundreds of people lining the road from his home at *Raddon Court* to watch the procession to Grappenhall Church. Conveyed by carriage, the mourners included Sir Gilbert and Lady Greenall, together with other local dignitaries from politics and industry.

Captain Reynolds built the mansion, *Raddon Court,* in 1883, near the tannery where he also erected a row of cottages for his workforce. The house has since been demolished and *Raddon Court 2000* occupies the site. A month before his death Sylvanus and his wife Jane presented the stained glass east window to Christ Church, Latchford.

To mark his services to the Conservative Association the members had subscribed for a marble bust to be sculpted by J Warrington Wood in Italy, whence it came, in the week that he died. Donated by his wife Jane in 1888, the bust was placed in the foyer of the Conservative Club's Sankey Street premises, where it remained until 1970 when the building was vacated prior to demolition.

The bust was purchased at that time by Mr Kevin Donoghue, in whose care it stayed until he generously gave it to the Conservative Club in 1992 — the 21st anniversary of the club's occupancy of Vigo House.

The Bust   *G A Carter*

TOWN BEGGARS

*extracted from the **Warrington Examiner**, 2nd June 1888*

As the halfway house between two populous and contending cities, the link between two important counties, and a stage upon a national highway, Warrington receives, retains and sustains more than its full quota of beggars. Whether from the gullibility, the soft-heartedness, or the timidity of its inhabitants, certain it is that in this busy and expanding town beggars are loth to leave its hospitable boundaries.

Watch the four main avenues leading into the borough any evening, Summer or Winter, and you will see entering the town with every conceivable variety of gait, such a motley assortment of weather-beaten, travel-stained individuals as will fill you with astonishment as to how they will find food and shelter.

On Saturday nights, Town Hill swarms with 'men on the road' and affords splendid opportunities for the study of human nature. Far-reaching odours emanate from the lodging houses, and tell of the good times the birds of prey were having — times far different to those of the genuine poor who fail to elicit the substantial sympathy the professional beggar knows so well how to obtain.

As town improvements have swept away the nest of dilapidated buildings that stood on Town Hill, the beggars' colony has migrated to Dolman's Lane, the policeman's happy hunting ground off Bridge Street. Here, any morning from nine to twelve o'clock, may be seen the 'gentry' who are 'working' the town, taking an airing previous to commencing the day's operations. The men lean lazily against the pillar that blocks the entrance of the lane to carts and take whiffs from stumpy clays with the air of self-satisfied persons. The women hang in groups about the lane corner, or stand about the footpath, and gossip with the vivacity of people who have a lot to say and little time to say it in.

BANKERS, BREWERS AND BENEFACTORS

Clare Furneaux

Between the late 17th and early 20th century, seven generations of the Lyon family held an influential position in Warrington and Appleton. In the years before the Industrial Revolution they were merchants and manufacturers with varied interests, including sugar refining and salt trading. As the century advanced they were less active in industrial processes but remained financially involved, while at the same time investing in property and land.

Brewing was carried on in all localities and at all levels of production, but the Greenall family expanded their operations from St Helens to Warrington. In 1786 William Orrett, Thomas Lyon and Thomas Greenall went into partnership to brew beer at Wilderspool. The name Orrett was withdrawn in 1807 and, when Thomas Lyon's nephew and successor (another Thomas) died in 1859, the brewery was left solely in the hands of the Greenalls until the Whitley family joined them in 1867. Brewing is no longer carried out at Wilderspool but many of the old buildings still dominate that historic site.

The principle of **banking** was a well established procedure, but with expanding commercial enterprise there was a pressing need to increase the capacity to manage money effectively. In 1788 another partnership was formed when Joseph Parr, Thomas Lyon and Walter Kerfoot became founders of a Warrington bank. Besides being in business together these three families had connections through marriage and, after Kerfoot's death, Edward Greenall joined the banking partnership and married a member of the Pilkington family (the glass manufacturers). In 1918 the bank, now called Parr's Banking Company Ltd, amalgamated with the London County and Westminster Bank and was named the Westminster Bank. In 1968 it joined with the National Provincial Bank and became the National

Westminster Bank (NatWest). Now in 2000, it is merging with the Royal Bank of Scotland. Its title has yet to be revealed!

Around the turn of the 18th and 19th centuries, **philanthropy** was in the air. Throughout the country, in spite of opposition from some landowners and employers who feared change to the existing social hierarchy, there were politicians and humanitarians who were dedicated to improving the lives of the underprivileged. The plight of chimney-sweeps and child labourers, together with conditions in factories and prisons, were among the targets for reform. The slave trade was abolished in 1833 as the result of many years campaigning and the Sunday School movement had a very large following in its efforts to spread literacy and moral improvement.

Like many other towns, Warrington had its share of both deprivation and social conscience. Thomas Lyon carried out civic responsibilities as a magistrate and a colonel of the Volunteer Corps. When he died in 1818 his nephew, also Thomas, continued in civic and business affairs, adding membership of the first Town Council and the Sanitary Committee to his list of duties. In 1855 Thomas Henry, the next in line, took the magistrate's oath and served as High Sheriff of Cheshire in the 1860s.

For well over a hundred years members of the Lyon family were Trustees of the Bluecoat School, which was set up to help families unable to cope with such hardships as unexpected bereavement, etc. The school benefited from their occasional donations and, in 1863, Thomas Henry also subscribed £20 to Warrington's Ragged School.

During the Crimean War (1854-56) Thomas supported the Patriotic Fund formed to aid the sick, wounded, widowed and orphaned as a result of the war. Members of the Warrington Police Force gave one day's pay and contributions were received from factories and individuals, from one penny upwards. This crisis was closely followed by the Indian Mutiny of 1857. Parr, Lyon & Co. were appointed bankers to the Indian Relief Fund, which was set up by a committee

VOLUNTARY
Relief Fund.

POOR PERSONS
DESIROUS OF OBTAINING
SOUP & COAL TICKETS

Are requested to give their Names and Address at the

National School Room, Church Street,

any evening (except Sunday) from 6 to 7 o'clock, and inquiry will be made, the day after, into their circumstances, by District Visitors, and Tickets given out by them.

Ladies and Gentlemen willing to assist in the taking of Names or in Visiting the Poor, are requested to attend at the National School Room at the above hour, or to give their names to the Rector or the Mayor.

The Committee will, in future, meet at the National School, (instead of the Dispensary) on Tuesday, Thursday, and Saturday evenings at 7 o'clock.

Parties buying Tickets for distribution, are requested not to give them indiscriminately, but only to such as they *personally* know to be in want. Others should be referred to the National School, or their Names and Address sent to the School, in order that they may be visited.

SOUP

is given out daily, (except Sundays) at the National School, Church Street, from 12 to 1 o'clock, on presentation of Tickets. Should any Soup remain after supplying parties with Tickets, it will be sold at the reduced price of One Penny per Quart.

COAL

may be had at half price, or 1½d. per half cwt., at Mr. May's, Foundry Street, Mr. Blundell's, Winwick Street, and at the Ince Hall Coal Yard, Dallam Lane. Coal will be also given out at the National School Yard, Church Street.

HENRY WHITE, Mayor, *Treasurer.*
WILLIAM QUEKETT, Rector,

Chairman of the Committee.

HADDOCK & SON, PRINTERS, WARRINGTON.

Advertisement dated 1854 -55, when Henry White was Mayor.

'deeply sympathetic' to the plight of the British men and women suffering in the Mutiny. Collections were made in churches and over £600 was raised. However, the fund had to be held in abeyance as the committee could not decide how it should be used!

In January 1855 both Thomas and his son, Thomas Henry, were appointed Trustees of the Warrington Dispensary, which provided treatment and medicine to needy patients. Thomas also subscribed to a scheme during this period whereby poor people who needed soup and coal had to give their names at the National School, in Church Street, between 6 and 7 o'clock every evening (except Sunday). The soup was given out daily at the school at midday and coal was sold half-price (3d per cwt.) at various venues.

The whole of Lancashire, including Warrington, was hit by the cotton crisis of 1861-65, brought about by the American Civil War. A national fund was set up, concerts were given to aid the local effort and Thomas Lyon was a patron.

The town's cultural life was well supported by the Lyon family. As subscribers and participants at dinners, balls, concerts and bazaars, they helped to raise funds for the museum, the music society, churches and hospitals. They served on committees responsible for maintaining highways, waterworks, savings banks and local agricultural shows. Of course they did not work alone; many others in Warrington were similarly concerned. As the 19th century drew to a close, the Lyon family and others like them had served the needs of the town for well over a hundred years.

MISS MARJORIE GRIFFITHS

Miss Marjorie Griffiths is well remembered as headmistress of Bewsey Girls Secondary Modern School. She was also a JP and was made a Freeman of the Borough just before she died in October 1994.

circa 1918

The photograph was taken outside Penketh Council School in Stocks Lane. It shows David Griffiths, her father, who was headmaster at Stocks Lane, with his family. Marjorie is on his knee.

TWO DISTINGUISHED ARTISTS

Cyril J Leake

Taken from Cyril's address to the Society when Chairman in 1993.

In 1855 the Warrington School of Art appointed Jonathan Christmas Thompson, then aged 31, as headmaster. He was a native of Carlisle, who had studied Art at the Royal Institution in Edinburgh and then at the School of Practical Art in London.

He proved an inspiring teacher, and soon students were attracted to Warrington from a wide area of the north-west. Because of his success, the museum building, which then housed the school, proved inadequate and, in 1882, John Crosfield headed the subscription list with a donation of £1,000 for a new specialised building.

Henry Woods, son of William Woods, a jeweller in Fennel Street, was a talented pupil. Henry was born in 1846 and showed an aptitude for drawing at an early age: by the time he was nine he was a part-time student at the School of Art, receiving his general education at Boteler Grammar School, where he remembered 'floggings were frequent.' The then headmaster, Revd. Henry Bostock, MA was also a painter in water colours and encouraged the boy's artistic ability.

In 1857, the Art School moved from the old academy building into the museum. In the same year, an exhibition entitled *Art Treasures* was held in Manchester. Henry Woods attended and recalled how impressed he was by the exhibits, which included Gainsborough's *Blue Boy*. In the same year Henry, still only 11 years of age, was awarded two national bronze medals.

In 1860, **Luke Fildes** became a pupil at the School of Art and he and Henry Woods quickly became firm friends. Luke Fildes was born on St Luke's Day, 18th October 1843.

Following his widowed mother's remarriage, Luke went to Chester to live with his grandmother. He attended Chester School of Art for some time, but received painting instruction from Alfred Sumner, a water colourist, who inspired young Luke with his love of Art. It was Sumner who encouraged him to enrol at Warrington's Art School.

In 1862, the two student friends went to the *International Exhibition* in London. The main building occupied a site of 16 acres, much space was devoted to Fine Art and both men were greatly impressed.

Back in Warrington, Luke discussed with Mr Thompson his wish to study in the exciting capital city and was encouraged to apply for a scholarship to study Religious Art at South Kensington. He won this and, in October 1863, set out for London.

At this time illustrated journals, such as *Cornhill* and *The Gentleman's Magazine* were flourishing, employing notable artists, including Millais, as illustrators. Luke thought such magazines offered a stepping stone to higher things because of their variety.

Whilst still a student Luke also produced sketches suitable for engraving, which were well received. This success decided him to work for the illustrated journals during the day, while he continued his painting at life classes in the evenings.

In December 1869 a new illustrated magazine, *The Graphic*, was launched, containing a full page illustration by Fildes entitled *Applicants for Admission to a Casual Ward*. On the strength of this, Millais introduced Fildes to Charles Dickens, who was seeking an artist to illustrate *The Mystery of Edwin Drood*. Fildes got the job and was commissioned to produced two illustrations for each of the twelve weekly parts. He read the manuscripts as they were produced and discussed future developments of the plot with Dickens in order to produce suitable illustrations. Unfortunately, Dickens died before the story was complete but not before he had revealed to Fildes the fate of Edwin Drood and the name of his murderer.

Luke Fildes visited the home of Dickens at Gad's Hill after his death and painted a study entitled, *The Empty Chair*. It proved a notable success and was reproduced as a supplement to *The Graphic*'s Christmas number in 1870.

Two years after Luke Fildes went to London **Henry Woods** joined him, having also gained a scholarship to South Kensington. He too joined the staff of *The Graphic* and became adept at book illustration for such authors as Victor Hugo, Charles Reade, Anthony Trollope and Wilkie Collins. In 1869 Wood's painting, *Evening in a Welsh Valley*, was exhibited at the Royal Academy.

In 1870 both artists took studios in a large house in King Henry's Road, near Regents' Park, in London. **Luke** had met Henry's two sisters, Annie and Fanny, in Warrington and, on one occasion when they were visiting the friends in London, he produced a sketch entitled *Hours of Idleness*, which included the girls and was published in *Once a Week* in 1869. At the suggestion of Millais, Luke made this the basis of his painting *Fair Quiet and Sweet Rest*. Fanny Woods is

On dangerous ground. An illustration by Sir Luke Fildes for The Mystery of Edwin Drood by Charles Dickens (1927)

shown sitting in a boat, her sister Annie, who became the wife of Warrington architect John James Webster, is standing, while Henry Woods is resting on the oars. (The second man in the picture was a professional model.) The picture was hung in The Royal Academy and was acclaimed *Picture of the Year*. It was sold to a well known dealer for £600 and currently hangs in Walton Hall.

The success of this painting, coupled with his reputation as a black-and-white illustrator, promised a secure financial future so, in 1874, he married Fanny Woods. He flourished and, in 1875 at the age of only 32, engaged the foremost Victorian architect, Norman Shaw, to design and supervise the building of a large house for him at Kensington, next door to Lord Leighton, who became President of The Royal Academy in 1878.

Meanwhile, **Henry Woods** was also successful. He exhibited at the Royal Academy each year from 1869 until his death in 1921 and never had a painting rejected. In some years five were hung.

In 1876 he went to Venice on holiday with Luke and Fanny. Captivated by its light and colour he returned there to live. He had a large studio built and his many paintings depicted the daily life of the people against a background of wonderful architecture.

His paintings were much admired, both at home and abroad, and he himself was popular with the Venetians, whom he loved to paint. Warrington Art Gallery have examples of these happy pictures.

Henry Woods

Fair, Quiet and Sweet Rest by Sir Luke Fildes

He became a member of the Royal Academy in 1893 and was also elected a member of the Venetian Academy, because of his love for the city. And it was in his beloved Venice that he was found dead with a brush in his hand on 27th October 1921.

Luke Fildes continued his successful career in London, gradually concentrating on portraiture. Following the exhibition of his paintings of his wife and Mrs Agnew at the Royal Academy in 1887, demand for his services as a portrait painter grew, but in 1891 he produced one of his best known pictures, *The Doctor*. This was reproduced in countless forms and, in 1947, was selected by the United States' Treasury as a tribute to the medical profession and printed on a commemorative stamp.

In 1893 he began work on a series of royal portraits, including King Edward VII in 1902, Queen Alexandra in 1905 and King George V in 1912. In 1906 he was knighted as a royal painter and in 1918 made a Knight Commander of the Victorian Order. He died in London on 27th February 1927, only six weeks before his wife.

THE PLAGUE HOUSE, LATCHFORD

David Forrest

On 10th June 1649 Richard Warburton married Ann Domvill at the church of Saint Mary the Virgin, Lymm. The next year he built a house in Latchford, in a lane later known as Wash Lane.

For many years there has been a belief that it was at this house that the plague visited the neighbourhood. This belief led to the house becoming known as *The Plague House* and this name replaced the title of *Round Step House* that was used in the mid 1800s.

There is no documentary evidence that this dreaded scourge visited Cheshire after 1647. The disease may have come to the town in 1645 and 1647. In the latter year a collection was made in the churches of London and Westminster for the poor people of Warrington but the exact nature of their trouble is not known.

During the last 150 years *The Plague House* has been of interest to many historians and writers. The first of these was Dr James Kendrick who, on hearing that the bones of three bodies had been discovered in 1843, decided, in 1852, to investigate the site.

After a brief search in Brown's Field behind the house, he located a shallow grave covered with a slab of sandstone measuring five feet long by two foot three inches wide (1524mm x 686mm). Under this he found the remains of a young man. As there was no sign of nails or wood he concluded that the body had been buried without a coffin. This suggested that he had been buried as soon as possible after death, a common practice with plague victims. There is no mention of the burial in the registers of St. Wilfrid's Church, Grappenhall, the local parish church at that time, so we may assume that the burial had probably been without the services of a minister.

The wall surrounding the front garden was of sandstone topped with semicircular coping stones and a small hollow was carved in one of the corner coping stones. It was the practice in many areas afflicted by plague to have such stones so that the depression could be filled with vinegar to disinfect any money placed there for neighbours to purchase food or other items for the inmates of the stricken house. Dr Kendrick purchased the stone from the owner and presented it to Warrington Museum, where it remains.

The house had three phases of development. When viewed from the front, the right-hand side was original, built by Richard Warburton. The timbers were heavier than those in the rest of the building and the lower corner of all the cross beams was ornamented by a dentile carving, giving the impression of a costly construction. On the gable wall, below the upper window, was a panel with R W 1650 carved upon it — the initials of the first owner and the date.

The Plague House

The left side of the house was added some years later and was not as elaborate, with thinner timbers and no ornamentation.

At the rear was a further extension of a much later date. The roof was not thatched but covered with heavy, thick slates. In the lane in front of the house, there was a stream with stepping stones. It probably disappeared in 1883 when the lane was paved with setts after many complaints about the flooding and mud that residents had to endure.

In 1853, the *London Illustrated News* contained an article about the house which stated:

> *The dwelling is an interesting specimen of the half-timbered house, now comparatively rare.*

And the following was found in *The Dawn*, a Warrington magazine dated 1906:

> *We have heard a rumour that the building is likely to change hands, and we sincerely trust that, should the rumour prove authentic, it will still be jealously preserved from alteration and permitted to remain as one of our most interesting local relics.*

In September 1928 the Education Committee bought land on which to build the Richard Fairclough School — now the Environment Agency. During the debate, Alderman Arthur Bennett, another local historian, made the comment, "I hope *The Plague House* in the vicinity will not be touched."

On Tuesday 5th May 1936, Warrington Borough Council discussed the now run-down house. Previously, it had been proposed that the original part of the building be restored and used as an auxiliary museum. This idea was rejected, as was another suggestion that the authentic part of the building be taken down and reconstructed in a town park. This procedure had been carried out in 1911 when the *Fox Inn* in Buttermarket Street had been stored in Victoria Park and then allowed to rot away. (See next article.)

At a meeting of the Health Committee it was recorded:

The Town Clerk reported that the Museum Committee had intimated that The Plague House in Wash Lane was not in a suitable condition nor of sufficient importance to be maintained permanently by the Council.

It resolved that a Closing Order be made under Section 19 of the Housing Act, 1930 (as amended by Section 83 of the Housing Act, 1935) in respect of No. 57, Wash Lane.

From that date the old house gradually became derelict. The doors were eventually broken down, allowing local children and others to enter. These activities probably worsened an already sorry state of affairs and, on 9th September 1957, the Highways Sewerage and Planning Committee of the Council recorded that:

The Committee noted the intention of Messrs Chadwick's Estates to demolish the property.

It should be noted that, despite its poor condition, the building did not give up without a fight. The bulldozer sent to raze it to the ground broke whilst trying to carry out its task. But, by Christmas 1957 the site had been levelled and only the garden walls remained. The front sandstone wall had been replaced during the late 1800s by one of brick construction, but the sandstone side wall still stands today.

The site, immediately across the lane from Christ Church, Latchford, is now the location of a pair of semi-detached houses, which were constructed in 1963 by Gerry Clough of Lymm.

BUTTERMARKET STREET — A TRIO OF INNS

Dorothy Sullivan

The Fox

Sited in Buttermarket Street, this is first mentioned in 1700. Then in 1879 the licensee was blacklisted for harbouring thieves and in 1883 his wife was fined for permitting disorderly conduct in 'a house frequented by the worst class of people in town.'

The inn was closed in 1983 and became a shop. It was demolished in 1917 and the timbers were numbered and put in Victoria Park for safe keeping. They are thought to have been burnt on the Victory bonfire of 1945.

Crown & Sceptre

Also sited in Buttermarket Street, this was listed in 1818 and, in 1888, was the 'worst conducted house in town, where the landlady defied police and brewer, and said she would do as she liked.' It was rebuilt in 1913 when the road was widened and was combined with the *Curriers Arms*. In 1946 four men were shot in the hotel, one died and one committed suicide. Closed in 1971, the building was then taken over by the Halifax Building Society.

Curriers Arms

This was yet another pub on Buttermarket Street and one of four side-by-side at the top of the south side of the street, the others being *The Wheatsheaf*, *The Fox* and the *Crown & Sceptre*. The *Curriers* was at the corner of Buttermarket Street and Bank Street and the earliest date we have for it is 1741. It had numerous other names — the *Bricklayers Arms*, *Dog & Partridge*, *Jolly Butcher* and *St Patricks* — and was closed in July 1893.

THE WORKHOUSE ON OLD CHURCH STREET

Dorothy Sullivan

Taken from the Warrington Examiner of 14th June 1913

In about 1850 the workhouse building was about as plain as a building could be. There was not a single beautiful feature about it. The three storeys each had eight windows and the only thing that relieved the plainness was an old-fashioned porch projecting over the door. The front was usually plastered over with bills announcing all sorts of events, together with notices from both police and the public.

The entrance hall was large and a small room off it was a waiting room. On its left was the boardroom and to the right was the dining room, with plain tables. Behind it was the kitchen and behind that was the big wash-house — a busy, steamy place on the many wash-days.

Market day on Church Street. The workhouse is the tall building on the right.

Behind the boardroom on the left was the children's room and behind that was the school-room where the 'workhouse boys' were taught. These rooms on the one side, and the wash-house and kitchen on the other, formed two wings, which ran out from the main building.

At the back was a large open space and garden, which could be reached by a passage that ran along the right-hand side of the building. Beyond the garden was the old Infirmary, which stood on Orford Street and the Dispensary was in Buttermarket Street.

The workhouse stood next to the Bulls Head Inn, which was thatched at that time. Beyond it were brick cottages. Then whitewashed cottages (some also thatched) extended up the street towards the National School. Williamson Square was considered a snug place to live and quite respectable.

The old women inmates wore white caps and looked very well. An artist could have painted some pleasing pictures of the old folk as they sat out in the sun or gathered round the tables for meals. The building was old and shabby but somehow looked appropriate as the home of these old folks. It was often nicknamed *The Bastille.*

MERSEY STREET, EARLY IN THE 20TH CENTURY

Mary C Miller

In the early days of the 20th century the people who lived in the area around Mersey Street, Warrington, formed a close-knit community. Most of the families lived in cottages, some of which opened on to courts with communal sanitary arrangements. The men found employment in the tanneries, wireworks and other factories which surrounded their homes.

A row of shops on Mersey Street catered for daily needs — a butcher, dairy, draper, newsagent, cobbler/bookie, pub and, dominating all, Richard Miller's grocery and cooked meat shop, presided over by Miss Teresa Miller, the elder of his two unmarried daughters. The large shop window displayed dry goods, tins of biscuits, pyramids of tinned fruits, soups, and much else. The freshly home-cooked meats

Outside the family's grocery and cooked meats business at 82, Mersey Street are Teresa and Alice Miller, with their niece Nora Miller. c1910

were placed in the bottom of the window: roast pork with stuffing; boiled beef and udder; ox tongue and 'savoury ducks' (pronounced 'savvory ducks'), which were balls of meat cooked in small cake tins.

Miss Miller was the 'Lady of the Manor' to her customers. Her advice was sought on health matters, money troubles and marital problems. She took a great interest in everyone, especially the children; she was godmother to dozens over the years. She also had many amusing tales to tell of incidents which happened in the shop. In person she was tall, and spare as she grew older, which adds point to this story.

When trade was bad, usually when men were on 'short time', she had a habit of sitting sideways on the ledge which gave access to the window, and surveying the street for any interesting incidents. One day in the school holidays a group of children gathered to look in the window. They began to amuse themselves by playing the well known game, 'I spy with my little eye something beginning with ...', in which one sets the puzzle and the rest try to guess the object and become the leader in their turn.

The game proceeded uneventfully for a time. It was a warm day and the shop door was left open. Miss Miller could hear all. Sitting in her accustomed position she began to take part mentally in the game. All went well until one boy who was 'on' floored them all with the initials MMBFA. No-one could guess, not even Miss Miller, and at last they had to admit defeat. The boy who had set the puzzle announced triumphantly ...

"Miss Miller's Big Fat A- - -."

Astonished and unbelieving Miss Miller rose to her full height, but the group had melted away, vanishing into Hall Street. Miss Miller had a sense of humour. She herself related the story to her own nephews and nieces.

9 MUSEUM STREET — A BRIEF HISTORY

M Sherrington and Dorothy Sullivan

One of a terrace of late Victorian three storey town houses, 9 Museum Street in Warrington has had a more varied and interesting history than many buildings of the same vintage.

The 1891 Census reveals that the house was occupied by George Venn and his family. Warrington born, Venn was a saddler and harness maker who was wealthy enough to employ two servants to look after his wife, mother and baby daughter. By 1908, according to the 'Warrington Guardian Directory' someone by the name of Atkinson was in residence but unfortunately no other details are provided.

Perhaps the most colourful phase in the house's past came with the arrival of Mrs Mary Davies, a native of Dublin who advertised 'apartments' to rent in Kelly's 1913 'Directory of Lancashire'. Over the next thirty years a rich mix of semi-permanent residents and temporary guests passed through the door of number 9.

Convenient for the railway station and the town's principal places of live entertainment - the *Theatre Royal* and the *Hippodrome* - the house attracted a regular clientele of music hall and variety artists, partly because the manager of the former establishment had rooms there himself and recommended it. Whether its status as a 'temperance hotel was a positive selling point is debatable, but its respectability was unquestioned.

Among the most famous visitors was the legendary **Gracie Fields** and her husband then, Monty Banks. At that time she was the highest paid female performer in the world and in the 1930s was, without doubt, Britain's most popular singing star, with a string of hit records to her name and a successful film career.

Ivor Novello is perhaps best known as the writer of one of the 1st World War's classic songs, 'Keep The Home Fires Burning', but he was also an accomplished actor. During his stay he occupied the first floor drawing room at the front (now sub-divided into two bedrooms) and brightened it up with several large silk butterflies, which subsequently saw annual service as Christmas decorations.

Another noteworthy resident was the internationally renowned opera singer, **Richard Tauber**. He steadfastly refused to use a microphone when performing, relying instead on the awesome power of his voice. It is easy to imagine the old house reverberating as he warmed up before going on stage!

During the 2nd World War the theatrical connection was severed with the death of the owner and sale of the property for £550 to The Warrington Catholic Aid and Rescue Society. St Joseph's Hostel was opened on 14th September 1944 and operated until 1991, with the assistance of the Daughters of the Heart of Mary. Since then the Sisters of the Poor Servants of the Mother of God have continued the work under the auspices of the Warrington and District Catholic Society for Welfare.

Originally conceived as a temporary home for girls in difficulty, St Joseph's Family Centre, as it is now called, provides support, advice and counselling for those in need, particularly those having problems with family life. It is a member of the Network of Access and Child Contact Centres, and has a chapel for prayer and reflection.

BEWSEY OLD HALL FARM

Gladys Davies (née Stephenson)

In January 1940 the Stephenson family moved into the farmhouse which adjoins the old hall. They had farmed in North Yorkshire and all the cattle, horses, sheep, poultry and implements from the farm, along with the household contents, were brought to Warrington station by British Rail. The cost was £160, which was much lower than the quotations for cattle lorries. The family also travelled on the train and, on arrival, the horses were brought out onto the siding and the trap was filled with all that was required to feed the animals, the family and any helpers.

I will never forget travelling up Crosfield Street, driving the pony with my brother sitting at the back of the trap holding on to three horses. Cattle and sheep were driven along later by helpers who met us at the station. Furniture containers arrived about 4pm that day and by 8pm all the beds had been put up and eight people slept in the farmhouse that night.

Sheep had not been kept on the farm in the past as it had been mostly arable, growing potatoes and cereals. The cows were milked that night by hand and this continued each morning and night until a milking machine was installed and a milkman was employed, delivering to the Bewsey Estate and surrounding area. The farm was soon being ploughed, grassland fenced in and all was well until the Americans came to Burtonwood.

We were amazed one day to see American officers and surveyors walking around the farm and were told that 40 acres would be used as an American camp, which would run right through the middle of our land. Mr Stephenson received £24 compensation for the inconvenience of having to go round the camp to the fields beyond it!

The noise of the aeroplane engines being tested night and day was deafening! Then there were the guns in the woods which were fired as German planes went over to bomb the Lancashire towns. The house had a spiral staircase and during an air raid we slept in the centre of the building where a strong pillar supported the stairs. We never had a hit but plenty of shrapnel fell when planes passed overhead.

Lord Lilford owned the farm and house, and his agent used to come round to see what improvements we had made. Part of the moat on our side was cleaned out to the right of the bridge; the water to the left was home to coots and moorhens. The house was built of handmade bricks, but I think all the windows were quite recent. All around the house were very small cobblestones and there were paths of flags to the archway, house doors and wash-house. We laid out lawns and gardens, and soon had it all looking very pleasant and colourful. In those days we had three men living in the house, who worked on the farm, as well as my brother and father.

We had an orchard which had about 40 fruit trees, mainly pear and apple. One Saturday during the war, a schoolboy friend picked pears and I sold so many (as in those days one couldn't buy fruit) that I collected £70 from children and people who lived nearby. We sold the produce non-stop all day.

I married in 1949 and left to live in Northamptonshire. In 1951 my brother and his wife went to farm in Shropshire, and in 1954 my parents retired from farming to live in the Lune Valley, near Lancaster.

We had an interesting and happy life at Bewsey Old Hall Farm. I enjoyed travelling to Liverpool once a fortnight to have lessons with Joseph Green, the concert pianist. During this time I taught music at Kirkfield, then spent seven years teaching at Newton Bank School before my marriage.

MEMORIES OF HEATHSIDE

Dorothy Gorst

The source of my memories is my childhood. I was born in nearby Edgeworth Street and, after attending the infants school at the bottom of Rolleston Street, progressed to the junior school—called *Heathside* as years ago there was a Warrington Heath, which is shown on old maps of the area.

Heathside School was quite old. Open since 1854, it was suffering somewhat from wear and tear when I attended it from around 1948 to the mid-'50s. Nevertheless it enjoyed a good reputation. In its earlier years, particularly around the 1880s, it had been a large school but over the years the pupil numbers had fallen as people moved out of town. Of the school itself I remember the three-foot perimeter wall, with iron railings on top through which my big sister used to pass me sweets as we played in the playground at playtime.

St Paul's, 6th Warrington, cub pack outside Heathside School, circa 1956.

The fire station was across the street and there was great excitement when the fire engine came out. I can still hear the bells clanging and see the firemen tenaciously hanging on while they pulled on their protective clothing. On other occasions they would run from the terrace where they lived alongside the fire station, dragging on their clothes as they ran. I recall an exhibition at the fire station and the firemen demonstrating sliding down the pole at breakneck speed from the recreation room above.

Of the teachers at school I remember Mr White, the headmaster, a kindly man who seemed, in retrospect, to be sympathising with us as he prepared us for the dreaded '11 plus' examination. Most of the lessons were on basic reading, writing and arithmetic, with some religious instruction, for we were a church school and, on certain days in the church calendar, we would walk in crocodile to St Paul's Church on Bewsey Road. I recall having milk at break-time, rushing home for a mid-day meal, then dashing back for afternoon lessons.

An exciting event was the arrival of Silcocks' Fair on the Potato Market, which was the open cobbled area between the fire station and the wall of the *Blue Back* public house at the bottom of Allen Street. The painted pub sign was of interest to us children for it depicted Warrington's early Volunteer Soldiers, in their colourful uniforms and holding their muskets. (See pages 82 and 89.)

At the end of *Heathside,* on the corner after the firemen's houses, was Mr Wakefield's shop, where he sold second-hand car components and accessories; it was packed with these from floor to ceiling. On the opposite side, on the corner of Leigh Street and Kendrick Street which took you to the Infirmary, was Mrs Holbrook's off licence, where we bought pop, crisps and sweets with coupons from the ration books. On the other corner was Mr Garven's, the newsagent, where we bought blank scrapbooks.

At the other end of *Heathside* was Flag Lane, which led to King Street and Sankey Street. At the bottom of Flag Lane *Marks & Spencers* had a storage warehouse where their big vans delivered goods and I can recall the large concrete unloading platform. Golborne Street branched off at the side of the school and led to Sankey Street, as it does today. In King Street was Mr Jackson's pet shop and a boy from there used to bring snakes to school! Also in King Street was St Alban's School, at the junction with Mill Street which led to the fish market.

The large open area opposite the potato market was Queen Street and there was a narrow entrance to the big market alongside another of Walker's public houses. Leading from Queen Street (at the bottom of Allen Street) was Brown Street, which is still there and takes you onto Bewsey Street, although the office of Frank Dillon, the bookie on the corner, has gone. I started work there after I left school and had trained at Mr Shirtcliff's Typewriting College, which stood near the corner of Bewsey Street and Froghall Lane.

Established 1917

Telephone Warrington 1505

TYPEWRITERS   TYPEWRITERS

ALL MAKES Sold, Exchanged, Repaired, Rebuilt
NEW & REBUILT MACHINES ALWAYS IN STOCK
SERVICE & MAINTENANCE

Typewriting and Duplicating of Every Description

BRITISH TYPEWRITING COLLEGE
(*Principal:* HAROLD SHIRTCLIFF)

74 Bewsey Street   :   Warrington

It is not easy to visualise the Heathside area now, even after such a relatively short time, for the multi-storey carpark, with its bridge across to the bus station, was built on top of it all. So much of the old, much loved Warrington has disappeared in the new developments.

WATERWAYS AND RAILWAYS

Henry Ashcroft

In the beginning was the **River Mersey**. Important as it became as an artery for east-west transport, it was the obstacle which it presented to north-south traffic which first influenced the development of Warrington. The ford at Latchford was the lowest crossing point of the river and it was natural that a settlement should be established a little way to the north, and this area still has the parish church.

Lower and later crossings were by ferry, of which the best known was the one made by the monks of Birkenhead Priory. However, it was a much later one between Runcorn and Widnes which was immortalised by Holloway as having a fare of twopence per person per trip or per part of per trip. Once the Mersey was bridged at Bridge Foot in about 1285, Market Gate became Warrington's commercial centre, as it still is, together with the surrounding area.

In the 17th century, the River Mersey was made navigable up to Warrington as industry (notably copper) began to grow. Bank Quay is not far from Bridge Foot as the crow flies, but is much further down the winding river and therefore more convenient for the import of industrial raw materials. Warrington thus grew from three centres — St Elphins, Market Gate and Bank Quay, and all three owe their selection to the River Mersey.

There had been ideas in the 1660s of making the Rivers Mersey and Irwell navigable up to Manchester but they came to nothing. Below Warrington, Thomas Patten was able to facilitate traffic for his copper works by removing fish weirs from the tidal river. In 1698 he was able to write that 2,000 tons of goods a year were sent to and from Liverpool — by modern standards less than a train load.

The growing need to reach Manchester led to the passing of the Mersey and Irwell Navigation Act in 1720. This allowed the making of locks and weirs in the river course, as well as *cuts* to short-circuit loops (known as *Eyes* in Warrington). The first such lock and weir was at Howley so that the river no longer reached the ancient ford at Latchford. Through navigation seems to have begun about 1740. Above Howley, the route was improved by Woolston Old Cut (1761) which was, in turn, by-passed in 1821 by Woolston New Cut between Martinscroft and Paddington.

Silting of the tidal Mersey below Howley led to the making of the **Runcorn and Latchford Canal** in 1804. It was locked into the Mersey near the present Kingsway road bridge. Its water supply came by a leet which, after 1821, was fed from the Paddington end of the Woolston New Cut and crossed the River Mersey by aqueduct. The route passed very close to the site of the Latchford ford and, east of Stockton Heath, it has been filled in and converted into a footpath.

Two other canals predated the Runcorn and Latchford one. **Sankey Navigation** operated between St Helens and the River Mersey from 1757. The Act authorising its construction permitted cuts to be made along the course of Sankey Brook but may not have anticipated one end-to-end cut. Thus it was really a canal and claims to be the first.

The Sankey Canal in 1831, with the Seven Arches Viaduct in the distance.

The **Bridgewater Canal** originally took coal from Worsley to Manchester, but its 'Runcorn arm' from Trafford via Lymm and Stockton Heath, was opened by instalments in the 1770s. Unlike earlier canals which ran along valleys, the Bridgewater crossed the Mersey's tributaries by aqueduct. To cater for high traffic density, it was all cut on one level, and remains so, even where coal extraction has caused land subsidence and necessitated the raising of embankments and bridges, especially in the Worsley to Leigh stretch.

The advent of railways brought competition but not an immediate decline in traffic; there was still a packet service for passengers between Warrington and Manchester in 1871. It had been proposed in 1837 that the Sunday packets should not run during the hours of divine service, which was to be achieved by starting the Manchester to Runcorn summer packet at 4am. In Winter, packets between Manchester and Warrington were to start at 7am and halt at Hollins Ferry or Flixton until 12.45pm.

The ultimate waterway was the **Manchester Ship Canal**. Opened in 1894, its construction is well recorded. It strained lodging accommodation in Latchford to the utmost and a tented hospital was needed. Numerous alterations were made to existing waterways. The River Mersey, between Bridge Foot and Walton, was diverted, with the new Chester Road constructed beside it. The southern bit of the old course was retained as a backwater and given a lock connection to the Ship Canal. These alterations cut the Runcorn and Latchford Canal, the eastern end of which was connected to the Ship Canal and the remainder kept only as an industrial water supply line. The idea that a Warrington dock should made around a further portion of the old course of the Mersey was abandoned in 1896.

Railways came early to Warrington. The Liverpool and Manchester line, opened in 1830, was the beginning of the intercity network, though neither was a city at that date. There was already a line between Bolton and Leigh, which was then extended to Kenyon to join the L&M. The next branch, in 1831, was the Warrington and Newton Railway, running from the junction now called Earlestown and entering Warrington beside Dallam Lane. Two branches in the town, to Bank Quay and Cockhedge, were authorised but not built.

The next southward instalment of the West Coast main line was the Grand Junction between Dallam and Birmingham, which opened on 4th July 1837. It had a Bank Quay station, but this was north of Liverpool Road.

The next completed line was from Chester. It was intended to continue to Stockport, which explains why it crossed the GJR near Moore and approached Warrington, as it still does, on the main line's east side. But in 1850 it was built only as far as Walton Junction, its trains running to Manchester Victoria via Bank Quay and Newton.

Meanwhile, a St Helens company had powers for a line between Garston and Warrington, and was expecting to continue this towards Stockport, using the unbuilt extension of the line from Chester. It therefore opened in 1853 only as far as a temporary station at Whitecross. To resolve the situation, a new company was promoted to extend the Chester line from Walton to Stockport with the St Helens' line joining it at Arpley. This new line created the Wilderspool level crossing, within 150 yards of which there had to be a station. The line was opened between Arpley and Timperley in 1854, as was the extension from Whitecross. However, signalling problems and disputes delayed through running from Chester.

By 1860, the Chester line was jointly owned by the LNWR and the GWR, and the LNWR owned or leased all the other lines in Warrington. They introduced three improvements in the 1860s. Until then main line traffic between Warrington and Wigan went north to Earlestown, then east along the old L&M to Parkside and north to Wigan. With the opening, in 1864, of a direct line between Winwick and Golborne Junctions, services were accelerated.

In 1868, a new Bank Quay station was built at its present site with low level platforms on the east-west line. This facilitated connections and allowed Arpley station to be closed. However, the requirement for a station within 150 yards of the Wilderspool crossing was invoked by the Council to enforce its reopening. The third improvement was a new line from the Weaver Junction to Ditton, which crosses the Mersey at Runcorn and keeps Crewe to Liverpool traffic away from the Warrington and Earlestown route.

The Cheshire Lines Committee completed the railway system in Warrington, with routes between Liverpool and Manchester or Stockport via Glazebrook. As authorised by the Act of 1863, its Warrington station should have been on Winwick Road, at the junction with Kerfoot and Longford Streets. However, in response to local pleas, the loop line and Central Station were made instead and opened in 1873. The originally authorised straight line between Padgate and Sankey Junctions was opened in 1883 for non-stop and goods trains. The Widnes loop and branches from Halewood to Aintree and Southport, and from Glazebrook to Wigan and St Helens, were also added but are now all closed and lifted.

When the Manchester Ship Canal was made, every line crossing it had to be raised and diverted. Latchford Station was resited.

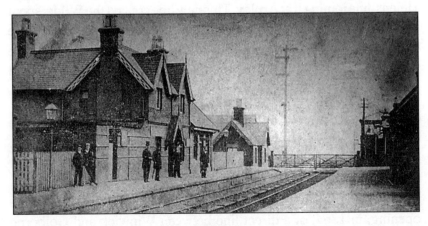

The original station at Latchford, circa 1887.

Dorothy Sullivan

The Packet House

In 1787 this inn was called the *Queen's Head* but is listed as the *Packet House* in 1821. Originally the inn had one entrance in Bridge Street and another in Mersey Street. On the corner was a shop occupied by William Woods and behind the pub were gardens and a summer house. It was sometimes known as the *Railway & Packet House* or the *Manchester Packet*. In the age of the stagecoach parcels would be brought up the River Mersey, deposited at the *Packet House*, then sent by coach to Manchester.

The Lion Hotel

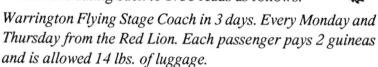

The Lion is one of the most historic pubs in Warrington. It was one of the first coaching inns in the town and an advertisement dating back to 1758 reads as follows:

> *Warrington Flying Stage Coach in 3 days. Every Monday and Thursday from the Red Lion. Each passenger pays 2 guineas and is allowed 14 lbs. of luggage.*

The present *Lion* was built in Bridge Street in 1759. The roof of the old building was part thatched and part slated and there were stables on either side. Originally known as the *Red Lion*, its name was changed to *The Lion* in about 1826.

A Happy and Sad First Occasion

J K Ashworth

For the Liverpool & Manchester Railway Company the day started as a day of celebration and pride in the announcement of their achievement.

In the forefront of the 'railway mania' which was to sweep the country in the early 19th century the Liverpool & Manchester had constructed a double track line between the two cities designed to carry both passengers and goods. The line passed north of Warrington, through Newton-le-Willows, and the instability of Chat Moss had caused the company major problems.

The previous year, in 1829, they had conducted the well known Rainhill Trials with a prize of £500. This was a competitive time trial for the fastest, most reliable and most powerful steam engine — the latter to cope with the steep gradients on the line. The competition was won by George and Robert Stephenson with their famous engine — the *Rocket*.

The *Rocket* had earlier been used in the Stockton to Darlington railway trials and had there achieved speeds of 12 to 16mph as a passenger service on a line constructed initially to carry minerals.

Stephenson's Rocket

15th September 1830 was the day of the official opening of the first timetabled railway passenger service. The initial run was to be by invitation of the directors, and included some very famous people, including the Duke of Wellington, who had been Prime Minister for the last two years; the Home Secretary, Sir Robert Peel; various members of Parliament such as Mr William Huskisson, MP for Liverpool; Lord Wilton; Prince Esterhazy, and various dignitaries of the two cities. This was to be a cavalcade of eight short trains — all pulled by Stephenson's locomotives, including the *Rocket*, the *Northumbrian* and the *Comet*.

Around the halfway point, about a mile east of Newton-le-Willows station, the cavalcade's progress halted to enable the engines to take on water. This took some time as the engines were manoeuvred in turn to the water point, and several passengers alighted to watch this and walk along the track.

William Huskisson had previously been a cabinet minister as President of the Board of Trade but promptly resigned in 1828 when Wellington became Prime Minister. Although they were both Tories some coolness still existed between them, but on this day, on the rail track, Wellington gave a sign of recognition and held out his hand. This friendly handshake was brief as a general cry of alarm was raised by some of the crowd. One of the locomotives, having left the water point on the down line, the people standing about, not being used to such speed, had to jump out of the way. Huskisson, having recently recovered from an illness, did not appear to respond quickly to the warning and was struck by the locomotive. Falling with his leg doubled across the line, he was severely injured.

An engine was immediately dispatched to Manchester to summon further assistance and Stephenson, driving the *Rocket,* took Mr Huskisson to the home of the Revd. Blackburn, Vicar of Eccles. Sadly, he died later the same day. This journey was a distance of nearly 15 miles which, we are told, was accomplished in 25 minutes at the record speed of 36mph.

The Prime Minister, in discussion with Sir Robert Peel, wanted to cancel the celebrations but was dissuaded from this on learning of the great crowds lining the last eight miles of the journey. The cavalcade, therefore, continued the journey but no music was played by the bands in attendance in Manchester.

15th September 1830, which started as a day of celebration, turned into a sad one. The day of the first timetabled railway passenger service in the world was the day of the first railway passenger fatality.

The Huskisson memorial now stands near the spot, on the south side of the railway and just east of the A573 road bridge over it. This is about half-a-mile outside the present Warrington borough boundary, just north of Hermitage Green.

A specific Warrington connection was the involvement of **William Allcard** (1808-1861). Born in Bakewell, Derbyshire, he became an apprentice/drawing office pupil of George Stephenson and, in 1826, Stephenson gave to Allcard, then only 18, charge of the problematical drainage and track foundation for the line's construction across Chat Moss. For the official opening Allcard was 'director' of the *Comet*, the final locomotive in the cavalcade, when his driver was John Robson and his fireman, Josh Richardson.

William Allcard settled in Warrington and bought Bank House in Sankey Street — the house next to the east drive to the Town Hall. In 1847 he unsuccessfully stood as Liberal parliamentary candidate for the town but was made an alderman in the first town council on its incorporation in that year. He became Warrington's second mayor in 1848, following William Beamont, then was mayor again in 1851.

We hear a lot these days about the long-term ill-effects of smoking and of smokers being asked not to smoke in public places. The problem is not new of course — as shown in the following extracts.

Smoking on the Railway

The directors of the London and South Western Railway, through their Secretary, have made an appeal to the common sense of the smoking public. They have determined to stop the practice of smoking in carriages, in consequence of the annoyance inflicted by those who disregard the rules on a great majority of travellers, not only while smoking, but also from the offensive state of the carriages to those who enter afterwards. The directors have invited the co-operation of passengers in discountenancing the practice of smoking on the railway, and they trust that those who, without due consideration for the convenience of others have violated the published regulations, will in future abstain from a habit which so much interferes with general comfort.

*from the **Liverpool Weekly Mercury**, 23rd November 1860*

Smoking Carriages on Cheshire Lines

A Liverpool merchant named Cooper, on Wednesday recovered from the Cheshire Lines Committee, the cost of cab hire which, after having booked himself and his wife as first class passengers, he incurred rather than travel in a smoking carriage. Mr Collier, judge of the Liverpool County Court, held that the railway company were bound to provide seats in a non-smoking carriage in that particular train for which the plaintiff had taken tickets.

*from the **Warrington Examiner**, 18th November 1875*

Proceedings of Council 31st October 1882

Motion

Tidal Navigation Scheme
Manchester Ship Canal

It was moved by the Mayor, seconded by Mr Alderman Burgess and resolved unanimously ...

... that this Council, having considered the scheme known as the Manchester Ship Canal for deepening, widening, and otherwise improving the Rivers Mersey and Irwell, so as to render them suitable for navigation by ocean-going vessels up to Manchester, hereby expresses its approval of the project, and pledges itself to accord every support to the scheme, provided the application to Parliament contains such provisions as will secure to this Borough and its inhabitants all the advantages to which, in the opinion of this Council, they are entitled.

The Manchester Ship Canal, with Latchford Locks in the foreground and Thelwall Viaduct behind.   *A E Howell*

THE OPENING OF WARRINGTON BRIDGE ON 7TH JULY 1913

Eric J Naylor

Details from Council Minutes of 12th August 1913 ...

At 3pm a royal salute of 21 guns announced the arrival of King George V and Queen Mary at Arpley Station. With their entourage, they drove in three open carriages along Arpley Road to Warrington Bridge, then along Bridge Street and Sankey Street to the Town Hall, where they were greeted by schoolchildren cheering and waving coloured flags, then singing the National Anthem.

After this the King opened the bridge by pressing an electric button fixed on the royal dais. Ingeniously, this severed a rope stretching across the north end of the bridge and a bell was rung at the bridge to announce the Royal Favour.

The royal party then visited the works of Messrs. Joseph Crosfield & Sons Ltd. Schoolchildren from the outlying districts of Stockton Heath, Grappenhall, Daresbury, Padgate, Orford and Sankey, lined the route over Bank Quay Bridge and crippled children watched from the broad footpath near the Town Hall's west entrance. The 4th Battalion of the South Lancashire Regiment (strength about 350) was also in evidence as was the Borough Police Force.

The Church Lad's Brigade, the Boy Scouts (four abreast) and the Pioneer Band then led the Mayor and dignitaries to Warrington Bridge, where the Chairman of the Bridges Committee, Alderman Smethurst, unveiled the plaque inscribed, THIS BRIDGE WAS OPENED BY KING GEORGE V — 7th JULY 1913. The party then crossed both old and new sectors before returning to the Town Hall.

The mayoral procession having departed for the bridge, the ladies entered the Town Hall and gardens, where light refreshments were served. A band played for dancing in Victoria Park from 7 to 9pm.

BEYOND THE BOROUGH BOUNDARY

John Dunabin

I was born in the middle of the 1st World War, less than three miles from Market Gate, but in those days Penketh was not part of Warrington, legally or in reality, and for many of its residents visits to town were something special.

Connor's horse bus to and from the village, packed to capacity I was told on Saturday nights, had been a wartime casualty — the army needed every horse it could get — and private cars were a great rarity. Even in the early to middle 1920s there was only a handful in Penketh, half of them chauffeur driven — no lifts from them! — so walking to Sankey Bridges, outpost of Warrington's trams, or even walking all the way, thereby saving one-and-a-half pence, was commonplace. We had our own shops of course, plus weekly deliveries of bread and groceries from town. There were regular visits by a hand-drawn piano organ too.

We had railway stations at Great Sankey ('Sankey for Penketh') and at Fiddlers Ferry, but both were some way from the centre of the village, and train fares were dear. My family was lucky in that we lived near Sankey station, a fact which now became important.

In the early postwar years teachers were very scarce and my mother, already on Warrington Education Department's books having taught in the town, was cajoled, by no less a person than the Director himself, Moore Murray, to return. The problem of what to do with a very small child was readily overcome and, at the age of just over three, I started at the new Oakwood Avenue School.

(Incidentally, all the D of E's persuasion would not have got mother back to her first school. Although it was strictly non-denominational she found herself the only nonconformist on the staff, under a head very well known for her aggressively High Church stance. The Director, though, knew all about this.)

Such matters were, of course, outside my awareness. Few memories of the school remain, apart from joining in the Empire Day celebrations, and being made to lie on the classroom floor (we must surely have had mats) for a period every afternoon. (It was received wisdom then that growing children all needed an afternoon nap.) More in mind are the journeys there and, even more, the waits *en route*.

The train from Sankey took us conveniently to Central Station (as now) outside which the cemetery trams terminated, end-to-end with those for Longford — specially open topped to pass under the railway bridge. On the west side of the street was Pendlebury's furniture shop, and each morning I watched the leisurely ritual of the opening of the two sets of workshop doors, one onto the street, the other mysteriously at first floor level. I could not understand what these were meant to protect. On the other side was Barlows' Corn Stores, much duller until

A tram at Latchford terminus in the 1930s. The last tram to run on this route was on 28th August 1935.   *M J O'Connor*

one day (a red letter day for me) when one window of the double-fronted shop was filled with a lively litter of small puppies. How I longed to take one home!

The tram journeys, trundling along Scotland Road, into Church Street and so on, should have been exciting, but again nothing stays in mind, or hardly anything. I did make friends with the tram conductors and one of them presented me with a shoebox crammed with tram tickets — the contents of the used ticket box no doubt. I carried the shoebox home in triumph, but then it mysteriously vanished. Puppies behind shop windows might be acceptable but grubby old tickets in the house? Never.

Then the employment situation changed as more men became available, and the authorities dismissed all their married women teachers. I changed schools and, instead of the train and tram journey, with glimpses of all sorts of things on the way, I had a walk along country lanes entirely devoid of human activity.

FREE GIFTS FOR ALL

J K Ashworth

We are all familiar with the '10p off' coupons by which the modern housewife can reduce the grocery bill by switching allegiance to whichever brand of corn flakes or soap powder is currently on offer. Promotional selling schemes for domestic goods are not new. They were introduced, in a different form, by the leading soap manufacturers in the early part of the 20th century.

The two leaders in this field were Lever Brothers of Port Sunlight and Joseph Crosfield & Sons of Warrington (now Crosfield Chemicals). Levers had their SUNLIGHT soap and Crosfields, their PERFECTION and PINKOBOLIC household lines — all three being the leading domestic brands of the time. It is interesting to note that both Lever Bros. and Crosfields had been close associates for some time. (Both were eventually merged, then became part of the Unilever Group on its formation in 1929.)

During their initial association Lord Leverhulme had always urged co-operation combined with friendly rivalry. Thus it was that the two major British soap companies, although associates, were in direct competition for the growing home trade market for domestic soaps.

The emphasis of the sales promotional schemes of the 1920s and '30s was not to tempt the housewife to make a trial switch of brands, but to encourage and persuade her to become a constant user of a particular brand. With this aim, the **Free Gift Scheme** offered a wide range of domestic goods in return for a specified number of redeemable coupons cut from soap packets.

During the difficult years following the depression of 1929, for the working class housewife to be able to obtain or replace any of the essential domestic items of the day, such as pots, pans, crockery, cutlery or towels, in a **Free Gift Scheme** was not only an added bonus but an essential part of her domestic budget. The pictorial literature produced in support of the scheme, showing the items available and their coupon value, gives a most interesting insight into the items of domestic ware of the 1930s.

Crosfield Free Gift Department gave employment in Warrington to a manager, assistant manager, two or three young men as administrative and clerical assistants and about 12 girls as coupon counters and despatchers, plus gift shop manageresses in Warrington and five other towns.

For most of the UK, a postal service was operated from the factory at Bank Quay and, in addition, about five or six local PERFECTION GIFT SHOPS were opened in Hanley, Hull, Manchester, Stockport, Wakefield and at 105 Sankey Street, Warrington. The latter (on the site of the Social Security offices at Hilden House today) was based there to be nearer the shopping area and save the public from having to go to Bank Quay.

Other towns, mainly in the North West and all within a day's travelling distance of Warrington, were served by a visiting Perfection Gift van, which was available on market days on a weekly or fortnightly basis at a regular pitch in the local market. The first van was a converted 10 cwt. Morris Commercial. Then in 1938 it was replaced by a specially designed Commer van, with specialised bodywork by Jennings, the coach builders in Northwich. This was a most impressive vehicle, with all the rounded contours of the 'streamlining' vogue of the 1930s. It did not have a long, active life in its original role, as the Free Gift Department was closed in 1940 for the duration of the war.

Advertisement kindly loaned from the archives of Joseph Crosfield & Sons Ltd.

Dorothy Sullivan

The White Bear

The White Bear was sited in Bridge Street and listed in 1787. A year later, in 1788, Peter Stubs leased the inn from Thomas Watt and the ale he brewed was deemed to be one of the best in town. He then started a file business and gave out work to file cutters. The files were covered with paste made from malt dust and the dregs of beer barrels, which preserved them from damage. He also established 'boxes' or funds , out of which payments were made upon sickness or death — an early form of insurance. The inn was closed in 1854 and purchased by Ralph Johnson, a cabinet maker, who turned it into a shop.

The Blue Bell

Known as *The Bell*, in 1792 it was sited in a little cottage on Horsemarket Street. At the rear was the Corn Exchange, a long room where property auctions were held and ground rents paid. The pub obtained its beer from Peter Stubs — reckoned to be the best ale in town. At one time the corner shop next door was occupied by Miss Cliffe, a milliner, then later by a hairdresser, James Ball. In 1874, however, it was knocked down and rebuilt as part of the pub.

THE BAY HORSE ON WINWICK STREET

Dorothy Sullivan

Situated on Winwick Street, the deeds of the *Bay Horse,* dated 1796, mention a summer house, garden and pin manufactory, partly used as a public house. The sale of 1855 describes it as an old established public house, with stabling, coach houses, brewhouse, outbuildings, fustian cutters' shop and yard behind.

George Formby (senior) was a friend of the proprietor, Thomas Roberts, and was a regular visitor to the pub. He presented a silver cup for fishing in 1918. His son George (junior) played with the children. He was sent to train as a jockey in Ireland but disliked it and fled back to the Bay Horse. It closed in December 1990.

List of people who occupied the cottages behind the Bay Horse in 1881:

Samuel Groom	James Reader
William Owen	John O'Brien
Ellen Makin	Peter Carol
James Johnson	Mary Cazene
Samuel Davies	Mary Mallom Hale
John Redfern	Ellen Laurence
Eliza Ridgeway	Thomas Cotton
Abram Humphreys	William Claw
Ralph Wood	Thomas Daintith

PUBLIC HEALTH IN WARRINGTON (1160 - 1950)

Dr P O'Brien

The first Boteler Lord of Warrington was born about 1160 and the family reigned for four centuries until the 18th Baron died in 1585, the population increasing from 120 to 2,500 in that time. Originally, the settlement was a mere village, on rising ground above the river, around the Saxon church of St Elphin. This gradually extended westward along Church Street and, although primitive, was healthy for its time. And so it remained until the community extended along Mersey Street and the low ground on the north bank of the river.

From then on public health became a problem as water lay all around. There was no sewerage apart from large, filthy open ditches, eventually emptying into the river, so that later the sector bounded by Bridge Street, Buttermarket Street and Mersey Street was dubbed Sewer Island. Other adjacent, low lying parts of the town were little better.

The domestic water supply was from numerous shallow wells in among these ditches, assuring regular contamination when these open sewers overflowed. The streets drained along central channels and the only toilets were middens. This was Warrington's scourge for generations and one that authority was criminally negligent in addressing, even when the Industrial Revolution brought wealth and employment here. Also, when other towns and cities had a variety of hospital care this town had none until early in the 19th century.

The famed Warrington Academy (1757-86) was an import, not looked upon too kindly by the townspeople, but it did raise awareness of medical potential. Its first pupil, Thomas Percival, was from a local family, whose grandfather, a surgeon apothecary, had provided basic medical care in and around the town, followed by his son, Thomas (1691-1750), who had studied at the famous University of Leiden in Holland (Europe's leading medical school at that time) and returned with his doctorate, conferred by Herman Boerhaue, a world renowned teacher. This Thomas Percival, MD served Warrington throughout his career. The younger Thomas was his nephew who, on leaving the Academy, went on to medical school at Edinburgh University, which was fast overtaking Leiden. On qualification, he returned to practise in Warrington, but only for six years, after which he moved to Manchester, where he had a distinguished career, becoming a consultant physician at the infirmary there.

One of Percival's contemporaries at Warrington Academy, although several years younger, was John Aikin, whose father was the Academy's senior tutor for most of its life. The son also went to Edinburgh in time and, after qualifying, went onto Manchester then London for further study, before returning to Warrington where he was in private practice and served as a part-time tutor at the Academy.

His particular achievement there was the teaching of students whose sights were set on medical studies. He offered these special tuition in anatomy, physics, chemistry and botany, following in the footsteps of Dr Joseph Priestley. These two between them prepared 22 students who went on to study medicine; 14 definitely went to Edinburgh (and probably 7 more) and one went to London. A number of these had distinguished careers and Aikin's contribution was highlighted in the first Medical Register published in London in 1779.

During these significant years a Warrington Improvement Bill was introduced in Parliament, one of its major objectives being to rid the town centre of its shambles, where butchers' stalls jutted out into the main thoroughfare, especially in Bridge Street, shedding blood and offal onto the public highway. This proposal provoked a tremendous outcry from those with a vested interest and we still have the evidence because they had their individual submissions printed by Eyres' Press. 28 items in all can be found in our local history library.

James Kendrick, MD, FLS (1771-1847) was born in Warrington during the latter years of the Academy. He drew inspiration from it and was the first local practitioner to move things forward. In 1810, together with other leading figures, he was responsible for founding the Warrington Dispensary, originally housed in leased premises in the Cornmarket until a new building was erected in Buttermarket Street, to which the establishment was moved in 1819. This fine building is still standing to the west of St Mary's Church. It catered for outpatients from the start, but in later years a house was acquired opposite, in Orford Street, where there was a small number of beds for inpatients. The staff consisted of a resident surgeon-apothecary with two apprentices. The resident medic occasionally went out to do house calls and a vaccination clinic for smallpox was held once a week. A nurse was later employed for inpatients and her contract was for cooking as well — all at £20 per annum.

Upstairs in the main building there was a committee room, a small museum and a library with a fine collection of medical classics. This library went missing in later years and finally surfaced with a second-hand bookseller in London, where it was spotted by Sir William Osler and purchased for the Johns Hopkins Medical School in Baltimore, USA, and McGill Library in Montreal.

By 1876 it was decided to build a hospital, which was erected behind the Town Hall at the junction of Legh Street and what was to become Kendrick Street. This **Infirmary and Dispensary** opened in 1877 and eventually had 170 beds. Dr John H Gornall, the last house surgeon in Buttermarket Street, was one of those who oversaw the transfer. The Infirmary was still Warrington's leading hospital at the start of the National Health Service in 1948. Until then it had been a voluntary establishment, maintained by a Workpeople's Committee. It finally closed in 1980.

In 1831 cholera arrived in Britain for the first time. Having travelled from northern India to Europe, the epidemic reached Hamburg in that year, then came by sea to Sunderland and gradually spread throughout Britain, arriving in Warrington in June 1832. By the end of September there had been 169 fatal cases. Not surprisingly, the heaviest incidence was in the area bordered by Mersey Street, Bridge Street and Buttermarket Street. A Board of Health, as recommended by the Privy Council, was set up towards the end of 1831 to prepare for the expected epidemic. Its secretary, Thomas Kirkland Glazebrook, produced a detailed and interesting report. In all, cholera came to Britain four times between 1831 and the mid '60s and it is remarkable, and surprising, that Warrington only had the one epidemic.

The first workhouse, established at the western end of Church Street in 1727, accommodated a few cases of cholera in the early stages, then later a small temporary hospital was provided in redundant premises on the south side of Mersey Street.

The Infirmary

Later, the workhouse was moved to open ground at the end of Guardian Street, south of the Cheshire Lines Railway, where it remained until the NHS arrived. At the southern end of this land, and to the north of Aikin Street, a fever hospital was opened in 1877, which was still in use during the early years of the NHS. A temporary hospital, set up in an old ironworks off Winwick Road to accommodate an epidemic of smallpox in 1892-3, was followed later by the smallpox hospital in Great Sankey.

In 1871 the Registrar General and the Medical Department of the Local Government Board became concerned about the 'sanitary condition of Warrington and the prevalence of fever in the town.' Dr Edward Ballard was despatched from London to study the problem and report back and there is no suggestion that Warrington was unique. Ballard was just one of a team, but it can only have been a small number of black spots that had this degree of attention.

Ballard's report, after his inspection in February 1872, was published in the Proceedings of Council in 1882. It gives the population of Warrington as 29,879 (24,050 in 1861) and the Death Rate as 30 per 1,000, with 'infant mortality much higher than it ought to have been.' He comments on the very poor housing — many small dwellings, back-to-back, with poor ventilation and drainage. 'The old fashioned midden closet is the one principally in use ... a source of nuisance and poor drainage ... the midden becomes a pestiferous faecal swamp.' One particularly bad example he gives was at a registered lodging house in Ship Yard, off Bridge Street, where the closet was close to the side wall of the house and opened directly onto the court in front. It consisted of a simple, upright slab of stone, behind which the excrement had accumulated nearly to the top. There was no seat, the floor was wet and filthy with urine and stools, and the stench from the privy was overpowering.

Main drainage in the principal streets was into brick sewers with outlets into the River Mersey at Bank Quay and a storm outlet at the bridge. This at least was an improvement on the large, open ditches of 1832. However, there were only about 300 to 400 water closets discharging into these public sewers. The piped water supply was also deficient and the quality bad.

Yet Ballard does offer some encouragement and compliments the Borough Council (established in 1847) for its response to the Local Government Act of 1866. He commented that the Surveyor, Inspector of Nuisance and Sanitary Committee were all striving to make improvements.

The recommendations Ballard made were:
1. Appoint a Medical Officer of Health.
2. Clear up excrement, refuse, etc.
3. Deal with midden closets and substitute water closets.
4. Provide effectual ventilation.
5. Improve the public water supply.
6. Put into place arrangements to deal with epidemics.
7. The Medical Officer of Health should deal with nuisance arising out of manufactures.

This was all very promising. Dr John H Gornall was appointed the Medical Officer of Health in 1880 and made his first report in February 1882. He was able to list some encouraging improvements over the decade, but even from then onwards some failings remained for a long time. Many of the smaller houses in back streets had no water closets and only outside dry closets. This state of affairs persisted into the 1950s, with the night-soil carts trundling along at breakfast time on their way to the sewage depot at Longford, the men sitting atop these carts munching their butties! This is within the memory of this writer.

BOTELER GRAMMAR SCHOOL

Dan Doherty 1915-97

*Dan Doherty was the much appreciated headmaster of Woolston High School until his retirement and in 1996 the new Humanities wing was named after him. He was also chairman of the Archaeological and Historical Society in 1985 when the subject of his inaugural address was **Boteler Grammar School**, which he attended from 1924 to '33, his name appearing with 180 others on the school roll of 1926. This article is based on his lecture, recorded in the Society's Minutes.*

The school was founded in 1526, four years after the death of Sir Thomas Boteler who had made provision for such a foundation in his will, it being his intention to establish a school, 'whereby men's sons might learn grammar to the intent that they thereby might better learn to know Almighty God.' The Foundation Deed empowered successive Lords of the Manor and holders of the Bewsey Estates to appoint an 'honest and discreet priest as Master'. A house in Bag Lane (now School Brow) was set aside for the Master. No fees were to be paid except for a penny to support a cockfight on Shrove Tuesday and a penny for drinks in each of the other three quarters. No scholar was to wear 'any dagger, hanger or other weapon invasive, other than his knife to cut his meat with.'

It was further laid down that scholars were to go 'two and two in processions on Sunday, Wednesday and Friday about or within the Parish Church singing the Litany and Responds.' In Winter they were attend church 'between six and seven of the clock' every morning and then immediately go to school, whence they were not to depart till five in the afternoon— or four at the discretion of the Master. In Summer they were attend church between five and six. Every year on April 27th, the Founder's death was to be commemorated by a special service, held in the parish church, 'at the costs of every of the said Schoolmasters.' The order of service was specific and included the collect, 'Deus simul spes nostra', which is the origin of the school motto 'Deus spes nostra' — God is our hope. The service is held to this day, but not paid for by the headmaster!

After they had been twelve months in Grammar the boys were to speak to one another 'at all times and in every place, Latin and no English' and no scholar was to take part in 'dicing or carding or other unlawful games.' Every scholar was to be ready to give the master 'his help and assistance to the correction of any other scholar' and if a boy dared to 'make any fray upon the Master' he was to be 'amoved for ever except the said schoolmaster be contented to keep him still.'

Sir Thomas Boteler, in addition to the 500 marks set aside for the foundation, bought further lands which, in a codicil to his will, he made the capital property of the school. These estates were squandered in the late 16th century by Edward Boteler, a great grandson of Sir Thomas the founder, but were eventually restored in 1607 after the efforts of Sir Peter Warburton who had married Elizabeth, one of Edward Boteler's two sisters. Hence, in 1608 new Foundation Deeds were drawn up and, under a succession of well qualified Masters, the school prospered. Close links were established with Brasenose College, Oxford, a number of Masters having graduated there. The Masters from 1687 to 1932 were all priests.

1687-1718   Revd. Samuel Shaw, MA

Samuel Shaw had been Master of Wigan Grammar School since 1676, where he improved (or rebuilt) the schoolhouse and premises. In 1691 Shaw became Rector of Warrington and was the first to hold the two offices conjointly. He did much for the church and, in 1697, built the square tower, which is shown on many old pictures but was pulled down in 1859 when Rector Queckett had the present spire erected. In 1709 Shaw concurred with Peter Leigh of Lymm in the foundation of Trinity Church, Warrington. He died in 1718 at the age of 68, after 31 years service, and was buried in the chancel of the parish church.

After the Revd. Samuel Shaw, the Revd. John Tatlock acted as Master for a short time until the Revd. Thomas Hayward took charge.

1720-57   Revd. Thomas Hayward, MA

Thomas Hayward was born in Warrington in 1695 and was the only old boy of the school to become Master. He was a graduate of Brasenose College, Oxford, and trained many excellent scholars, including the famous Dr Thomas Percival and Thomas Alcock from Runcorn, who graduated MA at Brasenose. Hayward died in 1757 after 37 years' service, and was buried in Warrington. His other claim to fame was that he had 16 children.

1757-1807   Revd. Edward Owen, MA

Edward Owen, who was born in 1728, was a graduate of Jesus College, Oxford, and came to Boteler from the Merchant Taylors' School at Great Crosby. He converted outbuildings into a dining room and bedrooms, rendering the house fit for the reception of boarders—which it never was before. He also blocked off the Roman road which ran by the school from Latchford to Winwick, then built his stables on it. Under Edward Owen the school became famous, boarders arriving from distant parts. In 1767 he was appointed Rector of Warrington. He remained a bachelor and, after 50 years service, died in 1807, aged 79. He too was buried in the chancel of the parish church, on the south side of Samuel Shaw's grave.

1807-14   Revd. Robert Atherton Rawstorne, MA

Robert Rawstorne was another Brasenose College graduate who became Master and Rector at the same time. However, several leading citizens applied to the Court of Chancery to test Lord Lilford's right to the patronage of the school and to secure a declaration that the offices of Master and Rector should not be held conjointly. Four years later Lord Lilford's right to the patronage was confirmed, in virtue of his holding the old Boteler estates, and the two offices were declared incompatible, so Rawstorne was deprived of the Mastership in 1814. He remained as Rector until 1832 when he left Warrington. He died at Hutton Hall, near Preston, in 1852.

1815-28   Revd. William Bordman, MA

William Bordman was officially appointed Master in 1815 after really being in charge of the school for seven years, for the Revd. Rawstorne left the entire management of it to him and allowed him to live in the schoolhouse. He was a graduate of Pembroke College, Oxford, and a somewhat hard man. He was once prosecuted, though without success, for 'immoderately correcting' a boy named John Booth. To his credit, in 1822 he started a proper pupil register. No earlier registers exist. He resigned in 1828.

1828-42   Revd. Thomas Vere Bayne, MA

A scholar of Jesus College, Oxford, in which city he was born in 1803, Bayne continued to keep the register begun by his predecessor. He introduced a school excursion each Spring or Summer, with an inevitable essay the next day and a prize for the best account. He helped the Rector of Warrington, the Hon. Revd. Horace Powys, to raise money to build the National Schools in Church Street — opened in 1833. He also saw his own new school erected in 1829, a school capable of accommodating 120 boys. Revd. Bayne resigned in 1842 to become Vicar of St John's, Broughton, where he died in 1848.

1842-61   Revd. Henry Bostock, MA

A graduate of Wadham College, Oxford, previously Henry Bostock had been Master of Aylesbury Grammar School. Under his leadership Boteler did well for ten years, then began to decline. Disorder crept in and pupil numbers fell off. Finally, when he accepted the chaplaincy of the workhouse in 1861, the Trustees managed to enforce his resignation. He retired to Southport where he died in 1863.

Before the next appointment, the Trustees decided to remodel the school buildings. The Master's house, which had probably stood since before 1526, was then pulled down in 1862, along with the 'new' school, built in 1829. These were then replaced by the building in School Brow. During the rebuilding some of the boys were sent to Winwick School, the Master of which, Revd. Henry Burnell, had formerly been an assistant master at Boteler.

1863-81 Revd. Offley Henry Cary, MA

In 1863 Boteler reopened under Revd. Cary of Christ Church, Oxford. It was he who engaged masters to teach accounts, mathematics, French, German and drawing. He also introduced the custom of an Annual Speech Day. In 1869 came the Endowed Schools Act, under which new schemes of management were devised. Such a scheme was drawn up for Boteler and received Royal Approval in 1880. Mr Cary resigned at Easter 1881 before the new scheme came into effect. He went to Devon and became Rector of Trusham, near Chudleigh, where he died in 1919.

1881-1907 Revd. Edward John Willcocks, MA

A graduate of St Catharine's College, Cambridge, Revd. Willcocks was appointed by the governors, who had replaced the trustees in the new scheme. The first issue of the school magazine, *Pincerna*, appeared at the beginning of Mr Willcocks' Mastership in 1882, but the next issue was not published till 1894 and there was an interval of eight years before the third! After that the magazine appeared regularly until 1914, when publication lapsed during the Great War and was not revived until December 1923. Mr Willcocks was the last Master to live in the schoolhouse, moving in 1905 to *Heathfield*, Latchford Without. He died there in 1907 and was buried in Grappenhall churchyard.

1907-32 Revd. Horace Gray, MA

Of Jesus College, Cambridge, Revd. Gray was a cricket 'blue' in 1894 and '95. He came to Boteler from Kendal Grammar School, where he was headmaster. Pupil numbers continued to increase and the school on School Brow began to feel cramped by the growth of industry around it. In fact, negotiations for a new site had started even before the War. 16 acres of land were purchased at Latchford in 1924 and it was hoped to have the new buildings ready to celebrate, in 1926, the 400th anniversary of the school's foundation. The design of the new school was thrown open to competition and the winning entry was the work of two old boys — Mr S P Silcock and his son, Mr H S Silcock.

A new sports' pavilion, partly financed by the subscriptions of past and present pupils, governors and friends of the school, was erected in time for the Anniversary but the building of the school itself had not even been started.

The problem was money, the cost being beyond the school's means. An agreement was eventually reached between the school governors and Warrington Education Authority and, in 1932, the inevitable had to be accepted — the independent status of Boteler would have to come to an end. Responsibility was transferred to Warrington Corporation, along with the school's financial endowments. Mr Gray decided to resign and Mr Price Evans, one of the assistant masters, became acting headmaster, a position he held until 1940. In that year the new building was opened by the Revd. Edward Downham, who had been Chairman of the Governors since 1934 — and in fact remained in office until his death in 1968.

The school roll in 1926 was 181 whereas in 1940 the new school had 350 boys on roll; a fact accounted for by the amalgamation of the old Boteler Grammar School and the more recently founded Warrington Secondary School. At the opening on 16th September, the Revd. Downham spoke of the unique task ahead with the merging of the two schools and the need to build on the traditions of the past.

The building which once housed Boteler Grammar School on School Brow.

The Marquis of Granby on Church Street

THE MARQUIS OF GRANBY

Dorothy Sullivan

Still thriving on Church Street, this historic inn was named after John Manners, Marquis of Granby. A popular English general from 1721 to 1770, he won fame during the Seven Years War (1756-1763) when Great Britain took Canada from the French. John Manners was a fearless and somewhat foolhardy soldier who, during one whirlwind cavalry charge, is said to have lost his wig. His bald head then acted as a guiding light for his men and this episode is said to have given rise to the phrase 'going at it bald headedly'.

The original sign for the Marquis of Granby is believed to have been displayed at Hounslow, by Sumpter, a discharged trooper of the Horse Guards, who the Marquis had commanded as a colonel. After the campaign the Marquis established his senior non-commissioned officers who had been disabled, as innkeepers.

Epitaph
Oh! where shall Britain make her boast
Or where display her banners?
Since now in Granby she has lost
True valour and good manners.

The earliest date for the Marquis of Granby in Church Street is 1768, but it is thought to have been built about 1660 as a gentleman's town house. In 1910 plaster fell from the west gable and it was revealed that the ancient timber frames were infilled with wattle, not bricks.

The Town and its Volunteers

Major (rtd) T J D Farrington

Warrington has had military connections for a very long time but the townspeople have probably showed their patriotism more than ever during the last two centuries. First, when the threat from France was at its greatest at the end of the 18th century, there arose a force which, with its successors, was to be intimately associated with the town ever since, namely the Loyal Warrington Volunteers (1798), familiarly called the *Bluebacks*. These, and their immediate successors, the *Robin Redbreasts*, were the predecessors, a few times removed, of the noble 4th Battalion Volunteers, the South Lancashire Regiment of the Territorial Army Militia, which came into being by the Militia Bill of 1757 which, when amended later, allowed Militia Captains to supplement the ordinary militiamen (who were compulsorily furnished *pro rata* by each parish).

It was not long before the Volunteers began to form themselves into independent Companies and when the threat of French invasion was at its height the Warrington *Bluebacks* formed up, with Edward Dakin as Captain Commandant and a strength of 160 men. There was no individual patriot but the unit emerged 'from the spontaneous desire of the gentlemen of the town of Warrington' and the necessary expenses were met by public subscription. An extract from 'The Bluebacks' states:

> 'that each man provided himself with arms, accoutrements, clothing and provisions, and that they laid aside all distinctions of private life: the shopkeepers, professional men and clergy took their places indiscriminately in the ranks, actuated by one common ardour.'

The Militia Battalions existed before and throughout the 1800s, until the Cardwell Reforms of 1881 turned them into Special Reserve

Battalions to feed the new Regular Army, that is, the newly named South Lancashire Regiment. This period was a time of British Colonisation when the Empire was being built and much of the Army saw service abroad, whilst the Militia were engaged in Home Defence and support to the Civil Power.

The foresight of Cardwell (Secretary of State for War) who abolished Commissions by purchase in 1871 and formed the twinning system for regiments in 1881, gave us our present county regiments' system. The 40th and the 82nd regiments of Foot were amalgamated and territorialised to form the South Lancashire Regiment. Cardwell saw the chaos which existed in the army at the time of the Crimean War in 1856, the Indian Mutiny in 1857/58 and the Maori Wars in 1860/66. Much of it was due to communication difficulties, for instance despatches to the United Kingdom from India and Australia took from six to ten weeks or more. The army was also overstretched and Volunteer Rifle Companies emerged in the mid-19th century.

These volunteers provided everything for themselves, from clothing and equipment to rifles and ammunition, and Lord Derby was a great benefactor in Lancashire. The 47th Lancashire Rifle Volunteers in St Helens also had great sponsorship from the Pilkington family. In Warrington the 9th Lancashire Rifle Volunteers were supported by the Fairclough and Crosfield families, and many others. These Rifle Volunteers were the predecessors of the new Cardwell system (1881) and, under the banner of Regimental Volunteer Battalions (VBs) Cardwell bonded them together, resulting in the 1st Volunteer Battalion, recruiting in Warrington and Newton, and the 2nd Volunteer Battalion from St Helens and Widnes.

These were so well trained that when volunteers were called for in the Boer War no less than 116 officers and men came forward to form three detachments, which fought alongside the Regular 1st Battalion South Lancashire Regiment in South Africa. The 4th Royal Lancashire Militia was also formed into a Special Reserve Battalion in 1881, principally to feed trained soldiers into the Regular Army, but such was the need in 1900 that it too went to South Africa for a short time.

The numbered infantry regiments of foot, prior to Cardwell's reforms had no loyalties to counties or towns. They moved from garrison to garrison, town to town, recruiting as they went. They had no barracks and were billeted on the local residents and in ale houses. They coerced and recruited the male population to join them, offering the sum of £5 (equivalent to £165 in 1998) for the recruit's signature or cross on his attestation papers for at least 12 years' service. The Militia being a local body, it had a barracks at the top of Crown Street, near the Cockhedge Mill. This still existed at the time of the Boer War, as evidenced by a letter from the Mayor to Lt. Col. Ridgway on 27th August 1897, sanctioning the use of the old Militia Barracks should mobilisation be ordered.

Casualties from the 1st Volunteer Battalions in the Boer War amounted to only a few killed in action but many more casualties resulted from disease such as dysentery, enteric fever, cholera, pneumonia and the like. Many were invalided home.

By 1908, the Volunteer Battalions had their designation changed to Territorial Force by yet another army reform attributed to Haldane, Secretary of State for War. The Territorial Force in Warrington produced six Battalions of Volunteers for the 1st World War.

Further change came in 1920 when the Territorial Army (TA) was formed. It is said that history repeats itself, and so it does, for when the Strategic Defence Review of 1999 took effect the Kings Regiment (TA) and the Cheshire Regiment (TA) were amalgamated to form the present Territorial Unit in Peninsula Barracks, of the Kings & Cheshire Regiment (KCR) (TA).

Returning to the true Warrington Volunteers, the old 4th Battalion South Lancashire Regiment was renamed the Lancastrian Volunteers in 1967, then the 5th/8th Battalion Kings Regiment TA in 1974.

All the Volunteers have been consistently supported by the townspeople, the more so in times of strife. When war was declared in 1914 the 4th Battalion South Lancashire Regiment was at its annual camp at Hornby in Lancashire. It was 'captive' and the order to mobilise was swift. Within five days 15 officers and 853 other ranks had volunteered for overseas service. Home Defence TA had no commitment to overseas service but could volunteer. The necessary equipment of horses, carts and wagons was hired locally to bring it up to war standard. By 12th September further volunteers had increased the strength to 31 officers and 1,342 other ranks. The same month the 4th Battalion South Lancashire Regiment, under the command of Lt. Col. Brereton Fairclough, a Boer War veteran, arrived in France fully trained and ready for war. A second 4th Battalion was raised from the flood of volunteers and went overseas under the command of Lt. Col. J D Fairclough, with yet a third (3rd/4th Battalion) being raised for Home Defence.

Eventually the Territorial Force was disembodied from 1919 onwards and was reconstituted as the Territorial Army in 1920. Parades were held in the Drill Hall, Bath Street, with regimental orders being posted each week outside the Town Hall.

In 1925 the name of Orford Barracks, built in 1878, was changed to Peninsula Barracks to commemorate the battle honours of the regiment in the Napoleonic Wars, and a few years later space was found in the Peninsula Barracks for a library and museum.

When war clouds gathered again in April 1939 the TA Battalion was duplicated once more, and so the 2nd/4th Battalion appeared. During the Great War 5,428 men were lost, whereas 864 were lost in the 2nd World War. More changes followed as a result of defence cuts; the old Drill Hall in Bath Street closed in 1964 as the 4th Battalion moved to the Peninsula Barracks. This, however, drastically shrank in size and eventually ceased to be the depot of the Regular Battalion. Peninsula Barracks, built in 1878 to prepare for the Cardwell reforms, had increased to 288 acres by the time a new cricket pavilion was built in 1922, but by 1969 it was only 17 acres.

Further changes occurred when the old South Lancashire cap badge ceased to be worn in 1967 and a collar 'dog' with the name 'Lancastrian Volunteers' came into being. Some of the old and bold were reluctant to change and the South Lancashire Regiment badge was still worn for some time. Also at this time the attached Army Cadet Force unit at Peninsula Barracks was not required to change its cap badge and so the old South Lancashire Regimental cap badge was still seen on the cadets too.

ROLL OF THE THIRD CONTINGENT.

No.	Army Rank.	Name.	Address.
	Lieut.	FAIRCLOUGH, B.	Barryfield, Latchford.
7148	Sergt.	THORNLEY, J. T....	10, Porter-street, Warrington.
7149	Corpl.	SEWELL; E.	49, Legh-street, Warrington.
7151	L.-Corpl.	GREEN, W.	56, Regent-street, Earlestown.
7150	Drummer	BRAMHALL, J.	27, Fairclough's Avenue, Warrington.
7152	L.-Corpl.	BLACKBURN, C.	7, Glasshouse-row, Warrington,
7153	Private	BIRD, J. T.	236, Manchester-road, Warrington.
7154	Private	BURROWS, A.	17, Dudley-street, Warrington.
7155	Private	CLARKE, E.	4, Heaton-street, Warrington.
7156	Private	CROZIER, J.	37, Lythgoe's-lane, Warrington.
7157	Private	DUTTON, J. H...... ...	8, Bluecoat-street, Warrington.
7158	Private	DAVIES, T.	15, Wellington-street, Warrington.
7160	Private	FORSTER, M.	19, Farrell-street, Warrington.
7161	Private	JOYNSON, S. ...., ...	30, Lythgoe's-lane, Warrington.
7162	Private	LITTLEWOOD, R.... ...	13, Howley-lane, Warrington.
7163	Private	LAWTON, W......... ...	10, Greenbank, Wilderspool, W'gton.
7164	Private	LEA, J.............. ...	4, Clare-street, Warrington.
7165	Private	LEWIS, G.	16, Manley-street, Warrington.
7166	Private	MORGAN, W.	148, Longford-street, Warrington.
7167	Private	McWHIRTER, W... ...	33, Albert-terrace, Warrington.
7168	Private	MORRIS, H. B...... ...	40, Elizabeth-street, Warrington.
7169	Private	OSBORNE, R.	38, Manchester-road, Warrington.
7070	Private	OXLEY, J.	22, Milner-street, Warrington.
7172	Private	ROGERS, A.	20, Fairfield-road, Stockton Heath.
7173	Private	ROUGHLEY, G....... ...	18, Parr-street, Warrington.
7174	Private	THOMAS, W......... ...	20, Eustace-street, Warrington.
7159	Private	WALSH, M.	5, York-street, Warrington.
7176	Private	WADE, G. F.	52, Sharp-street, Warrington.
7178	Private	WHITFIELD, H.	237, Wilderspool-road, Warrington.
7177	Private	WOODHEAD, J.	3, Hughes-street, Warrington.
7175	Private	WHELAN, J......... ...	29, Fairclough's-avenue, Warrington.
7171	Private	RICHARDSON, A.... ...	Victoria-street, Stockton Heath.

(Died at Heidelberg, from dysentery, May 7th, 1901.)

More changes in 1974 meant that the Lancastrian Volunteers became the 5th/8th Battalion Kings Regiment and the Army Cadet Force changed its cap badge to the Queens Lancashire Regiment. It should be noted that, prior to ththis, the South and East Lancashire Regiments had been amalgamated in Hong Kong in 1958 into the Lancashire Regiment (PWV), then joined with the Loyal North Lancashire Regiment at Dover in 1970 to form the Queens Lancashire Regiment.

History was made in 1947 when the town bestowed the Freedom of the County Borough on the South Lancashire Regiment (both Regular and Territorial) which meant they could march through the good old town with colours flying, drums beating and bayonets fixed. This honour, having been exercised by successive regiments ever since, initially occurred annually, but with financial constraints and operational duties the last freedom march of the 20th century was in 1998. This has now been followed by one in October of the Millennium Year 2000. The Queens Lancashire Regiment is extremely proud of this exclusive honour handed on by its predecessor, the South Lancashire Regiment, and not granted by the Borough Of Warrington to any other regiment. In spite of changes to the county boundaries the Queens Lancashire Regiment still recruits successfully in the Warrington area. Long may it do so.

In 1994, the Ministry of Defence withdrew grant aid to many museums, which were then forced to amalgamate, as the regiments of infantry had previously done. This eliminated the very last trace of the South Lancashire Regiment in Warrington. However, all its artefacts and archives are now housed in a new museum block at Fulwood Barracks, Preston. This is open to the public, free of charge, five days a week, and open to groups by appointment.

Acknowledgements
The archives of the South Lancashire Regiment
Lt. Col. (rtd.) E J Downham, MBE, BA
The Regimental HQ Queens Lancashire Regiment,
Fulwood Barracks, Preston, PR2 4AA. Tel: 01772 260362

THE OLD BLUE BACK

Dorothy Sullivan

In 1798 local Volunteer Regiments were formed throughout England, as there was a threat of invasion from France and unrest in Ireland. The Old Blue Back Regiment, formed in Warrington, was the second in Lancashire. When Napoleon heard about Warrington's Old Blue Backs he decided not to invade England and turned his attention to Egypt — or so the story goes! The regiment was disbanded in 1801 and two years later a new regiment of volunteers was raised — the Robin Redbreasts.

The *Old Blue Back* inn was to be found on Allen Street in Warrington and the earliest record of the beer house there is in 1861. Sadly, the building was demolished in 1993. One of the inn signs, showing three Blue Backs, was painted by Mr Reg Rimmer, curator of Warrington Museum. The inn's name is unique.

WARRINGTON, 16th March, 1817.

Mr. NICHOLSON regrets extremely that he did not pay proper attention to the two **WORTHY GENTLEMEN** who visited his House last Night, and hopes that on any future occasion, when they may feel inclined to repeat their visit, he shall be more prepared to give them such a reception as they are entitled to expect. In order however to prevent accidents, he begs to say, that as

SPRING GUNS

And other means of annoyance are now set about his Premises, it may probably not be safe for them to approach his House by the Way they did last Night.

HADDOCKS, PRINTERS, WARRINGTON.

Family History and Waterloo

Mary C Miller

In researching family history a maiden aunt is invaluable. She will relate family incidents and compile a dossier of newspaper cuttings of births, marriages, triumphs and tragedies. My mother's elder sister, 20 years her senior, was such a beloved aunt and I, the youngest of five children, sat at her knee and imbibed knowledge of the family reaching back to the late 18th century.

I learned that my great-grandfather, a sergeant in the 33rd of Foot, the Duke of Wellington's own Regiment, fought at Waterloo in 1815. His young 17-year-old wife, Ann, an Irish girl carrying her first son, accompanied him to the battlefield to attend to his domestic needs, as was the custom in those days. I knew that he suffered deafness as a result of the noise of gunfire, but survived otherwise uninjured and accepted his discharge without pension as he had a business to inherit.

In later years his money diminished and his son applied to the MP for Nottingham, who then contacted the War Secretary, Gathorne Hardy, and he received a pension until his death.

His son, William Madin, my grandfather, by now living in Liverpool and working as a compositor on the Liverpool *Courier*,

George Madin

celebrated his own Diamond Wedding in 1910, when his father's story was recalled and the newspaper account preserved by my maiden aunt reads ...

'Mr Madin's father, George Madin, had a long and honourable military career and was a survivor of Waterloo. He enlisted in the Notts. Militia in 1810, from which he volunteered into the 33rd of Foot, and took part in the storming of Bergen-op-Zoom, the force being under the command of the Duke of York where one of the British regiments laid down their arms. After this disastrous campaign, the 33rd Regiment was sent to join the force under the Duke of Wellington, and took part in the engagements at Quatre Bras and Waterloo. When peace was proclaimed, he accepted his discharge on the reduction of the army. He returned to Nottingham and followed the business of his father, a butcher, and by his careful habits saved a little money for himself and his wife in their old age, independently of any claim on the government for military services. He retired from business and lived on his little accumulation.

Old age creeping on, and his means of subsistence diminishing, his eldest surviving son William, laid his father's claim to a pension before the Secretary of War, Mr Gathorne Hardy, stating the plain facts, and at the same time informing him that he had never made any claim for services rendered to his country whilst in prosperous circumstances.

The application was acknowledged within seven days, and the son received a memorandum to be filled up and forwarded to the Commanding Officer of the Nottingham district. This was done, George Madin answering all the questions put to him, even to the names of his front- and rear- rank companions at Waterloo which, after such a length of time and when he was in his eighty third year, was remarkable. The Secretary of War then granted him 10/6 a week from February 1874, paying him £16.10s down, the 10/6 a week to be drawn monthly.

He died on 28th December 1874, aged 84 years, and is buried in Nottingham General Cemetery. I have not seen the grave myself but believe that it records that ...

> 'He was sergeant in the 33rd of Foot under Lord Wellington and fought in the actions of Quatre Bras and Waterloo.'

An elderly cousin, who visited the grave some years later, reported that a laurel wreath was placed on the tomb on the anniversary of the Battle of Waterloo — by the Regiment presumably.

At Apsley House in London, which is a Waterloo shrine, I have seen his name, Sergeant George Madin, inscribed on the Regimental Record Boards of the 33rd of Foot.

I have a photograph of him as an old gentleman and a coloured one of his wife, Ann, as an old lady, with my beloved maiden aunt as a little girl of ten leaning against her knee.

The little girl, much loved maiden aunt, Sarah Annie Madin, lived to be 80 and was buried on my 16th birthday. I inherited a wealth of information from her diaries and address books, and I too became a maiden aunt. So cherish all maiden aunts if you are interested in your own family history.

In Affectionate Remembrance of

George Madin,

Who died December 28th, 1874, aged 84 years.

He was Sergeant in the 33rd. Foot, under Lord Wellington, and fought in the Actions of Quatre Bras & Waterloo.

" He was a loving Husband, a kind Father, and a sincere Friend. "

Historical Notes of Warrington RLFC

J Manley

The game of rugby, considered by many to be the greatest game in the world, takes its name from Rugby public school in Warwickshire. There it was created in 1823, when a student, William Webb Ellis, decided to handle and run with the ball, then was tackled by the opposition. The students considered this a great idea and it became an immediate success, even though the first applied rules were sketchy.

The game spread to other public schools, was played by the professional classes and attracted lower social classes, especially in the north of England. The Rugby Union was then formed in 1871, and standardised the rules throughout the game.

The game has been played in Warrington since 1876 and the Warrington Club was formed in 1879, when local teams Padgate and Warrington Zingari joined forces. The move to Wilderspool in 1883 consolidated the club and its first success came in 1886 when it won the South West Lancashire Trophy.

The participants in the game in the north were mainly working class — very different from the southern players — and it was the northern lads who found it difficult to cope with the loss of earnings to play the game. The Northern Union authorities applied to pay the players for their loss of pay — not a weekly wage, but compensation. The problem proved to be social, economic and political.

The trouble reached its climax on 29th August 1895, when representatives from 21 clubs attended a meeting at the George Hotel, Huddersfield. The clubs were: Batley, Bradford, Brighouse, Broughton Rangers, Dewsbury, Halifax, Huddersfield, Hull, Hunslet, Leeds, Leigh, Liversedge, Manningham, Oldham, Rochdale Hornets, St Helens, Tyldesley, Wakefield, Warrington, Widnes and Wigan.

At this important meeting a momentous decision was made. All clubs, with the exception of Dewsbury, opted to resign from the English Rugby Union to form a Northern Rugby Union, in which legitimate payment for loss of work would be allowed. The new legislators retained all the basic rules of Rugby Union for the first season and the 'broken time' payment was settled at 6/- (30p).

The first paying birthday of the new Northern Rugby Football Union was on 7th September 1897. More clubs joined and the new league started its fixture list on the first Saturday in September, a week before the official opening of the Rugby Union season. The English Rugby Union made stringent rules against the so-called professionalism, banning any clubs in membership from playing against Northern Union teams.

During the first two seasons the game was played in accordance with Rugby Union rules: 15 in a side; the same system of scoring — a try 3 points, a conversion 5 points; drop goal or goal kicked from a fair catch or from the field-of-play 4 points; a penalty goal 3 points. The scoring system was changed to 3 points for a try and 2 points for all goals in 1897-98.

The beautiful Challenge Cup, first presented in 1897, is considered to be one of the best £60 worth of silver ever purchased. Batley were the first winners of the trophy, beating St Helens 10-3. Warrington were defeated in their first final in 1901, 6-0 by Batley at Leeds, with an attendance of 29,563, but won in 1905, 1906, 1950 and 1954 after a replay at Bradford before 100,000 spectators.

Challenge Cup

Now the Wire!

Dorothy Sullivan

My father was a member of Warrington Rugby League Club and had a season ticket for the stand. When the war ended and rugby started again, I used to wonder what it would be like to go to a match. From our house we could hear all the cheering and shouting. My brother John, who was six years older than me, had a season ticket too but he didn't go very often.

Brian Bevan

One day, while I was still at Our Lady's Junior School, my Dad suggested that I went with him to see a match. I was thrilled. It was one of the local matches. I can't remember which one but I think Rylands Rec. was one of the teams. I thought it was great. My Dad then said I could go with him to a 'proper match' and I can remember going to see Warrington play Liverpool City. I was hooked! Unfortunately, I could only go to matches against the bottom teams when the attendance wasn't high!

In 1947 I started at the Girls High School in Palmyra Square (now the Borough Treasurer's office) and met Irene Barber from Beamont School. She went to the rugby matches with her aunt and uncle, who lived near the ground. They offered to take me to Wilderspool and my Dad agreed. I can remember the first match I watched with them. We stood in front of the scoreboard; it was fantastic! We then went to matches both home and away, visiting most of the grounds in Lancashire and Yorkshire.

I loved the shouting — "Knock on! Forward pass! Send him off!" I remember a match at St Helens when the man in front of us (a Saint's supporter) turned round at one stage when I was shouting and suggested I went home and did the washing up. I was annoyed!

Brian Bevan was a big hero of mine and, I think, of everybody elses. He would come onto the pitch looking as though he was going to collapse at any minute, then he'd get the ball and was away. Nobody could catch him. When they unveiled his statue near St James' Church a man watching the ceremony said to me, "He didn't look like that, did he?" "He certainly did!" I replied.

Another character was the scrum half Gerry Helme, an expert at Ju Jitsu. He was only small, but big forwards running towards him to push him out of the way would suddenly find themselves flat on their backs! Later the Rugby League banned this.

Opposite: Warrington Wires. The winning team of 1953-54.

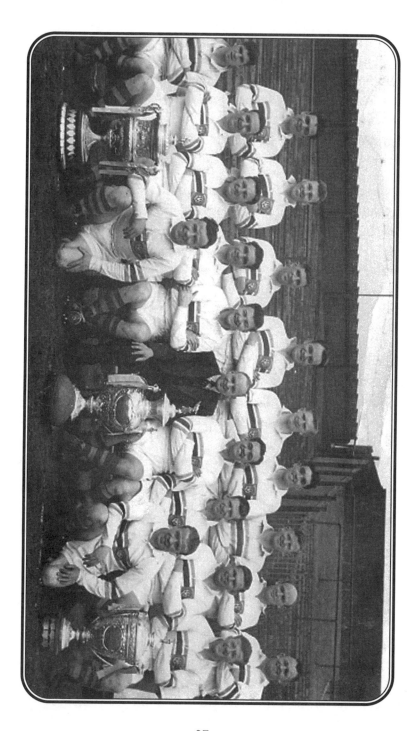

To go back to my younger days ... In 1954 Warrington reached the Cup Final, which was against Halifax, and we went by coach to Wembley. It was a great day out but unfortunately the result was a draw, 4-4, so there had to be a replay at Odsal Stadium in Bradford. We booked on a very smart Sykes Coach and left for the match on 5th May. On the Pennines in Yorkshire (this was before motorways) the coach broke down and we were very despondent.

As we were standing about, a rather old coach from Oldham approached and one man flagged it down. He asked the driver if he'd any room and some of us got on. When we joined a very long queue of coaches with nothing coming towards us on the other side of the road I can remember the driver suddenly going down the right-hand side to the front of the queue. On our arrival in Bradford, we parked about a mile from the ground and, after thanking the driver who had been so kind, we set off for Odsal.

At last we got in the ground and stood right up near the top of one of the corners. There were no terraces as they only went halfway up the embankment! Jim Challoner had already scored a try, so Warrington were in front. Gerry Helme scored at the end where we were standing and, although we couldn't see, how we cheered! It was a fantastic game, there was no crowd trouble and everyone was very friendly.

This was the match when, before the start, there was a request for silence for an important message concerning a party of altar servers accompanied by their Curate, Father Fraser from Our Lady's Church, Latchford. They had arrived with packed lunches and drinks, and Timothy Riley was asked to examine his bottle of milk as he'd taken a bottle of liquid starch by mistake. The ground erupted with laughter.

To return to the match, Warrington won 8-4 and, after the presentation of the Cup we had to find some way to get home. We walked past all the coaches asking if there were any spare seats for Warrington. At last we found some and left for home. It was a day I shall never forget, when I was one of a world record crowd of over 102,000.

MORE MEMORIES OF THE WIRE

Sandra Brookes (née Barnes)

Harry Bath, our goal kicker, once wrote to my father from Australia, addressing the envelope simply 'Reg Barnes, Warrington, England' and he received it. My father was a club director and, on retirement, sold his shares to Brian Pitchford.

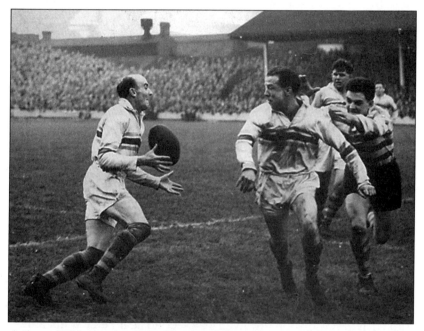

Action at Wilderspool — Brian Bevan and Gerry Helme, with Harry Bath behind.

The Britannia

Originating at 63 Buttermarket Street, *The Britannia* was rebuilt on the corner of Scotland Road, then demolished and incorporated into New Town House. Famous licensees of the pub were Harry Bath and Albert Naughton — captains of Warrington Rugby Club in the 1950s and '60s.

Public Timekeeping in Warrington

Kit Heald

At the beginning of the 21st century, the events of our days are kept in order by timepieces. At one end of the scale there are clocks which keep time to an accuracy of one second in three million years while at the other end we can buy a watch for a few pounds and regard it as an item to throw away when fashion changes. As well as our clocks and watches we can find out the time by reference to the telephone, television and computer.

Mankind has not always needed to know the time to such accuracy as we do now: in centuries past work was regulated by day and night, and the seasons. Even when clocks became more common they did not tell the same time uniformly throughout the country: that only came about with the railway system, when trains ran to a timetable. However, there was a period in between when the majority of the population did not have clocks or watches but did need to reckon the passing of time. This is when public timekeeping came into its own.

Time is Precious. Peter Winstanley erected this dial 1756.

... So read the inscription on the stable wall in the yard of The Bull's Head, Bridge Street — not quite the first public timepiece in Warrington but one that gave you a little reminder every time you looked at it. It was soon followed by a second near Peter Winstanley's residence with another adage,

Virtue join precious Time. The gift of Peter Winstanley
to the Publick in Stanley Street Warrington 1757.

Inscriptions on timepieces are not always inspiring or even visible. In 1647, Colonel John Booth gave the town possibly its first public timepiece — the **curfew bell**. It originally hung in a tower on the cornmarket and bore this inscription, *Donum Johannis Booth Colonelli et rectoris hujus de Warrington 1647.* (The gift of John Booth

Governor of this market town of Warrington 1647.) Beamont's record of the inscription is somewhat different being, *Exdono Johannis Booth armigeri Colonelli et rectoris emporii de Warrington 1647.* It later became the fire bell and later still was transferred to the clock in Trinity Chapel.

A variety of different dates are given for the move to Trinity Chapel. Beamont says that a bell with this inscription was put in the steeple there in 1706 but adds that the old curfew bell was also in the steeple. This other bell bears the following inscription, *Deo et ecclesia dedicavit Johannes Blackburn SSTP Hallelujah Henricus Penn fecit 1706.* (Consecrated to God and the Church, John Blackburn SSTP Hallelujah made by Henry Penn 1706.) A newspaper article suggests it was moved in 1810. If either of these is correct it would have been moved again after the steeple was blown down in 1822.

However, the minutes of the Police Commissioners for the town on 19th August 1841 contain a resolution that Messrs Joseph Perrin, Peter Smith, John Smith and James Houghtin be appointed a committee to make an agreement with the Trustees of Trinity Chapel to move the fire bell to the top of the steeple if practicable. Yet another source says that it wasn't transferred to the town clock (in Trinity Chapel) until 1855 when the old court house, where it had been, was demolished.

It is known that a new fire bell was hung on the west end of the new Market Hall when the building was erected in 1856. I suspect that these items refer to more than one bell and, although we may not be able to disentangle which bell was where during these years, it seems that the town authorities were taking an interest in public timekeeping.

On 21st April 1836 the Police Commissioners decided that the salary of the ringer of the Town Bell at 6am and 8pm should be paid by the Treasurer as, 'a matter materially attending to the regulation and order of the town'. In April 1863 Hamlet Savage was the ringer of the bell at a wage of 3/- (15p) per week and was given explicit details of the times for ringing it:

5.55 - 6.00am	Monday to Saturday
7.55 - 8.00am	Sunday
8.00 - 8.05pm	Every evening the bell was rung for 5 minutes then there was a break followed by ringing the number of the day of the month.
10.45 - 11.00pm	Saturday (in addition to the earlier evening ringing.)
9.45 - 10.00pm	Sunday (in addition to the earlier evening ringing.)

The Town Clock is housed in the tower of Holy Trinity Church, Sankey Street (built 1760). The first official reference to it is in the same Police Commissioners' minutes referred to previously (21st April 1836) when Mr Carter tended his bill for one year's care of the clock: from May 1834 to April 1835 the bill was 2 guineas (£2.10). The Commissioners ordered that this sum should be paid by the Treasurer as, like the ringing of the Town Bell, 'it was a matter materially tending to the regulation and order of the town'. James Carter's own notebook shows that, in 1824, he had previously received payment for work on the clock. As the steeple of Trinity Chapel (as it was called until February 1870 when it became a parish in its own right) was blown down in 1822 the clock was probably put in when the replacement tower was erected. Unfortunately, James Carter does not give us any other information about the clock.

The next official mention is on 1st February 1849 when Mr Carter reported that the winding ropes were 'so worn as to be dangerous'. (James died in 1848 so this must be one of his sons, probably Joseph.) The price of new ropes was to be ascertained and we can only presume that they were bought.

In 1852 more work needed to be carried out and Mr Carter was authorised to effect repairs not exceeding 45/- (£2.25). New ropes for the weights were supplied by Mr Wagstaffe for 28/- (£1.40) and to complete the improvements Mr Whittle repaired and repainted the dials at a cost of 10/- (50p).

Warrington's splendid town clock, atop Holy Trinity Church at Market Gate.

In the *Warrington Guardian* of Saturday 14th August 1858 there is an interesting report of the debate of a resolution at the previous week's council meeting. Councillor Holmes put the resolution that it was desirable to provide an illuminated public clock for the convenience of the inhabitants. He suggested that the matter should be referred to the General Purposes Committee to ascertain the best site for such a clock and an estimate of its cost. The important word is presumably 'illuminated' as there was already a town clock, but why was the councillor thinking of another site? Councillor Pickmere provided the answer when he said that Mrs Houghton's shop almost shut off the view of the clock from Market Gate. He believed that Market Gate was the only place for a public clock as anywhere else would only serve one locality whilst Market Gate was the true centre of the town. His suggestion was that a clock should be suspended on chains from the four buildings at the corners of Market Gate and have four faces, one towards each of the principal streets.

Councillor Holmes thought that the current clock could be made 'a yard or two higher' and, if illuminated, would be visible from more places than if it were put on any other public building in the town. He estimated that the cost of installing illumination would be £50 to £80, with running costs dependent on the length of time it was lit. Councillor Edelsten did not think it was the right time to be spending money on an illuminated clock but if one was really essential it should be sited at one end of the market shed, with one face to Market Street and the other to the market hall.

The resolution was sent to the General Purposes Committee and at their September meeting the borough engineer, Mr Coxon, was requested to obtain information as to the cost of maintaining the proposed clock. At the October meeting he reported that much depended on the size and situation of the clock. A clock on a pillar similar to the one opposite the Electric Telegraphic Company offices in Castle Street, Liverpool, would best answer the purpose and might be placed with advantage at the corner of Market Gate at the angle in front of Messrs Picton and Hattons.' This would cost £70 to £80, with maintenance of £5 per annum. The committee resolved that it was not prepared to approve Mr Coxon's plan and no-one seems to have resurrected Councillor Pickmere's suggestion!

However, it was not long before the council was forced into action. In November 1861 Mr Coxon reported to the General Purposes Committee that the dome of the clock tower in Trinity Church was much decayed and it would be prudent to cease ringing the bell. He suggested that the trustees should have it repaired or replaced. A builder, Mr Gibson, advised the commissioners of the chapel that it should be replaced, but they did not have sufficient funds to do this.

The rector, Mr James Nicholson, on behalf of the commissioners, approached the Corporation, pointing out that in the past matters of this nature had always been met by the inhabitants of the town generally as 'it is especially devoted to the town clock and the bell.' He promised the Corporation the commissioners' full co-operation. The General Purposes Committee then resolved that Trinity Chapel was the best site for a public clock for the convenience of those passing through the town and the following January the commissioners of the chapel offered £50 towards the cost of rebuilding the tower, which was accepted, and the total cost estimated at £200.

Councillor Edelsten, of whom we have already heard, offered the council a clock to be put up on Mrs Houghton's shop at Market Gate, if Mr Wilson, the owner, agreed. He said, 'he would take care that it was such a clock as would be not only a credit to himself but useful to the town.' It was to be made by Mr George Blackhurst, a Warrington clockmaker, and be guaranteed for 12 months. He asked that the Corporation should pay him 1/- (5p) per year as acknowledgment. A sub-committee was set up to confer with him. However, there seems to have been some ill-will between the members of the sub-committee, and Councillor Edelsten wrote to the General Purposes Committee complaining that they would not accept it on his terms but only under certain conditions. 'I am astonished,' he wrote, 'and after the uncalled for remarks ... the Corporation must accept the offer as it stands or decline it altogether.' The Corporation declined it.

Warrington Museum has a regulator with winders dial which is stated to be part of George Blackhurst's town clock of 1855, which came from Hamlet Houghton's shop. However, it is the wrong year if this was Councillor Edelsten's clock. There is no mention of this clock in the minutes of the General Purposes Committee and from the subject matter it undoubtedly would have been mentioned if it was there in 1858 or 1861. It seems then that either the date is wrong and Councillor Edelsten put up a clock notwithstanding the sub-committee's views, or this was merely a large or turret clock that was on Houghton's shop and calling it the 'town clock' is incorrect.

In April 1862 the Committee accepted tenders for work on the clock tower: Richard Kitchen, iron work £160; John Jackson, masonry, joinery and scaffolding £85; H & S Chandley, painting £8.

In August of that year the Committee, as ever trying not to spend more than was absolutely necessary, asked the Gas Company to illuminate the dial free of charge. The Gas Company's reply, in which it took no responsibility for the safety of the clock, was to agree to the illumination but with a meter from which £7.10.0 (£7.50) per half year would be deducted. By September it had been firmly decided that the old clock could not be repaired and that a new one was to be purchased. In October J Bailey & Co. of Manchester had their tender of £255 accepted for the construction and erection of a new clock.

By May 1863 there was dissatisfaction with Bailey's work concerning the clock. Some of this frustration is shown in the following verse which appeared in the *Warrington Guardian* of 30th May:

> Dithery, dithery dock
> What's up with the trumpery clock?
> It tells nothing but lies
> You don't know how time flies,

Unless by the Borough Reeve's clock,
And that tells the truth like the giver;
On both you may safely rely,
So three cheers for J B now and ever,
And three groans for the clock in the sky.
(Mr Edelston was the Borough Reeve.)

The real problems are seen through the minutes of the General Purposes Committee. In May 1863 the Committee gave Bailey's 14 days to finish the clock or the contract would be cancelled. Bailey wrote agreeing to this but did not do the work. Next Mr Coxon was told to have the work carried out by some other firm and charge it to Baileys. However, this does not seem to have happened either, because it is not until August 1864 that we are informed that Baileys had completed the work 'according to contract' (!) and £300.16.4 (£300.84) had been paid, with £45.16.4 (£45.84) being for extra work on the dial and telling hammers. Unfortunately, the minutes supply us with no more information about this strange state of affairs.

In July 1871 the old clock, which had been taken from the tower, was requested for use by St Paul's Church to 'provide a clock for the people at that end of the town' and the Committee agreed to hand it over to Dr Massingham as long as the Corporation incurred no expense.

January 1876 saw a new lighting system used on the clock. Arnold & Lewis of Manchester set the jets further away from the dials, where they gave a brighter light and ensured the dials would stay cleaner. The cost was £20 per dial, exclusive of joinery and ventilation work, and in May £92 was paid to the company, for the work and some other repairs. £15 was also paid to Henry Holt for painting the tower, which was next painted in 1881, when Mr Whittle was paid £20.

Another new clock was placed in the tower in April 1883. Made by Mr Joyce of Whitchurch, Mayor John Crosfield presented it to be put in Holy Trinity Church, and it was accepted with none of the antagonism that surrounded Councillor Edelsten's proposed gift over

20 years previously. James Joyce was a highly respected clockmaker who had made, among other turret clocks, one for Worcester Cathedral. In July of the following year the minutes tell us that the Corporation asked the company to provide an estimate for the care and repair of the clock for the following three years. In that same year the rest of the clocks belonging to the Corporation were put into the care of Mr Edward Eustance for their repair and winding, and he was paid £10 per year for three years. In 1886 it was also arranged with Joyce to fit new opal dials to the Town Clock.

After the dark years of the 2nd World War, the *Warrington Guardian*, on 28th July 1945, reported that the clock and tower were to be painted and pointed respectively. The possibility of adding more lights was to be considered and an attempt would be made to clean the faces from the inside. The ironwork was to be scraped and the figures and weather vane were to be gilded. It was mentioned in this report that the tower from the church roof upwards was regarded as town property. The *Warrington Examiner* of 8th August 1952 reported that in 1948 the clock and tower were overhauled as the weather vane, having attained a list of 5°, was thought to be a danger to the public.

Other well-known clocks in Warrington have been the market clock in the old covered market and E & A Eustance's clock above their

premises in Sankey Street, which could be seen there for many years. An advertisement in the *Warrington Guardian* on 26th November 1862 used the words 'The Illuminated Clock' with their name and address.

It was finally removed in 1993 when the firm moved into the Golden Square and, unfortunately, seems to have disappeared from public sight.

THE BIRTH OF THE CIRCULATING LIBRARY

Sylvia M Wright

In 1760 Warrington Academy, described by one author as 'a forerunner of the modern university colleges, and an 18th century centre of scientific and literary activity', had been flourishing for three years.

Two other institutions of note came into existence about the same time. Eyres' Press was unrivalled in Lancashire and further afield, for the quality and quantity of its output. Many works written by tutors at the Academy were printed there. Also, the Warrington Circulating Library was founded in 1760 and William Eyres became its first librarian, remaining in the post for 33 years.

This library was housed at Eyres' Press, a black-and-white, timber building in Horsemarket Street, and quickly grew into a fine collection of books, used mainly by tutors at the Academy, who also served on its committee. Among the names of the first committee we find Dr Seddon, Thomas Percival, three members of the Gaskell family and a Mr Thomas Bird — a poet from Blackbrook.

The committee met monthly for supper at *The White Bull* or *The Woolpack*, but they must have been a serious group as it was five years before a novel was purchased and, according to the minute book, only three were ordered in 10 years. After William Eyres, Mr James Haddock, also a printer, held the post of librarian for 25 years.

The library existed for almost 80 years then, with the passing of the Museums Act in 1845, it formed the nucleus of the Warrington Municipal Library — the first rate supported library in the country.

The Circulating Library, founded by those men of culture and vision, started a thread that has continued through 240 years and exists today in our present library, which still serves local people as an educational and recreational institution.

Towards Organised Local Government

Eric J Naylor

In considering the evolution of Local Government in Warrington it is necessary to look at what prevailed before William Beamont led his campaign to take advantage of the opportunities created by the 1832 Reform Act and its sequel, the 1835 Municipal Corporation Act.

We are inclined to think that the escalating crime wave and associated era of excessive violence is peculiar to our period in history. Not so, for mounting crime in the early 14th century led to the institution of Justices of the Peace. From then on, parliament consistently extended the powers and duties of the magistracy so that, by the end of the Middle Ages, the burden of Local Government fell on its shoulders. Elizabeth I put her faith in the JPs to contain the violence and worst excesses of lawlessness, which were attributed to the hungry and unemployed poor.

Domestic legislation was then concentrated on the Poor Law and so the Elizabethan Labour Code and Poor Law enactments were added to the statutes, the administration of which was the responsibility of the Magistracy. The magistrates, in fulfilling their duties, had recourse to the Parish Vestries, Overseers of the Poor, Surveyors of Highways, etc., but it became increasingly difficult, even in the 18th century, to provide the local services required. So, the many bodies of Local Commissioners were set up by special Acts of Parliament.

The 19th century was a period of great reform and more local services came into being. Separate organisations were created for each new service. The idea of an all-purpose local authority, however, had not yet dawned. In 1813 an Improvement Commission was set up in Warrington after an Act for 'Paving and Improving the Town of Warrington and for Building a New Bridewell' received Royal Assent on 3rd June. The Commissioners were to meet at the house of

William Hughes, the *Nags Head* inn (renamed the *Queen's Hotel* in Sankey Street and only demolished in the 1930s). This 1813 Improvement Commission named 23 commissioners, together with all JPs (both present and future ones) and everyone receiving rents of £40, or renting a house of yearly rental of £50, or with a personal estate of £1,000. There was no precise number of commissioners and all that was required to join the list, having the necessary qualification, was to swear the required oath before two commissioners.

An epidemic of cholera in 1831 led to the formation of local, temporary Boards of Health, with a central Board to guide and supervise them. In 1834 parishes amalgamated into unions, each with its elected Board of Guardians subject to the overall control of a body of Poor Law Commissioners. In the end, the setting up of so many separate bodies resulted in a most confusing pattern of authorities. There where School Boards, Burial Boards, Highway Boards, Sanitary Authorities and Poor Law Unions. Such a profusion of authorities was nothing short of an administrative nightmare. On top of this, the 1813 Improvement Commission had, as the years rolled on, become so large that William Beamont claimed it was unmanageable and started the movement to acquire municipal status, which had been available since the 1835 Municipal Corporations Act.

At a meeting of the Commissioners on 23rd February 1846, with John Clare in the chair, 224 commissioners attended and the meeting, held at the police station, had to be adjourned and moved to the Town Hall — a larger venue. (At an earlier meeting, on 19th February with 113 commissioners present, 64 new commissioners took the oath and that meeting had also had to be adjourned.)

Of interest, at a meeting on 19th March 1846, with Mr Rowson in the chair, after considering smoke nuisance from Rylands Factory in Church Street, a letter from a Mr Turner was read out asking for his name to be erased from the list of commissioners, as he had been mistaken as to the amount of his landed property. There was, of course, a penalty of £40 under the Act for false representation, or acting without having taken the oath.

William Beamont had, however, quite a struggle to get his fellow commissioners to agree to petition parliament for the grant of a Charter of Incorporation. There were many commissioners' meetings, as recorded in the minutes, with voices raised against obtaining such a Charter. Eventually however, the Commissioners resolved that the subject should be referred to a meeting of the inhabitants to take the subject into consideration, almost a referendum you might say! Following this, Peter Haddock, one of the constables who had been instructed to call the public meetings, reported to the commissioners that the meeting had been held at the Town Hall and that the following resolutions had been adopted:

1. THAT in the opinion of this meeting a Charter of Incorporation which should give to the Borough a more effectual self government by means of officers responsible to their fellow townsmen and to the public, would be a great advantage to Warrington and be calculated to promote its advancement in good order and prosperity and that this meeting is therefore of opinion that an humble petition should be presented to her most Gracious Majesty from the householders, praying that she would grant her Charter for Incorporating the Parliamentary Borough of Warrington.

2. THAT the following gentlemen be appointed a committee to carry into effect the foregoing resolution, namely Messrs Pierpoint, Guest, Beamont, Milner, Marsh, Allen and Hadfield with power to add to their number.

A further Warrington Improvement Bill had been under consideration at the time and so, at that meeting of the commissioners, it was moved by Mr Allcard and seconded by Mr Molineaux that, as a Charter of Incorporation would afford the best means of Local Government the proposed Improvement Bill be no further proceeded with, and that the Improvement Committee be instructed to co-operate with the committee appointed at the town's meeting yesterday to take measures for the presentation of a petition to Her Majesty in Council for the granting of such a Charter. This motion was eventually carried.

The Charter was granted, receiving Royal Assent on 3rd April 1847. This was in the 10th year of Queen Victoria's reign, which fact was incorporated in the first official emblem as seen over the Town Hall gates. The 'Anno decimo Victoriae Reginae' was, however, not included in the coat-of-arms granted in 1897, nor in the second coat-of-arms granted after reorganisation in 1974.

The Charter laid down that the first election of councillors should be held on 1st June 1847, and it charged Benjamin Pierpoint (who, in 1849, became the third Mayor) to make out the Burgess List, which was publicly exhibited in the manner of our Electoral Registers to this

1797 1889

WILLIAM
BEAMONT
HISTORIAN ANTIQUARY
AND FIRST MAYOR
OF WARRINGTON

PRACTISED HERE AS A
SOLICITOR FOR 50 YEARS

THIS TABLET WAS ERECT-
-ED IN 1913 BY THE
WARRINGTON SOCIETY

day. Lists of claimants and objectors to the Burgess List were drawn up and John Dakin Gaskell, Barrister at Law, was appointed to revise the Burgess List accordingly. The Royal Charter further appointed William Beamont to act as Returning Officer at the first election of councillors. The first meeting of Council was on 9th June, when the aldermen were elected, and the Mayor was chosen from the aldermen and councillors. The first Mayor was appropriately the renowned William Beamont, solicitor, local historian and town benefactor, whose efforts culminated in the Charter.

The composition of the Council, as declared in the Charter, was nine aldermen and 27 councillors. The Borough was divided into five wards, their precise boundaries being defined and named after the four quadrants (North West, North East, South East, South West) and Latchford. The four first mentioned wards were each to return six councillors and have two aldermen assigned to each. Latchford ward was to return three councillors and have one alderman assigned to it.

The Mayor and Council walked the Borough Boundary on 10th September 1847. This old custom of *Beating the Bounds* was partly revived on the 50th Anniversary of Incorporation in 1897, by which time, following two boundary extensions, the Borough boundary was about eleven miles!

The numerical composition of the Borough Council remained the same up to its demise in 1974 on the reorganisation of Local Government, although the ever expanding town had by then been divided into nine wards, each returning three councillors and having one alderman assigned to it.

William Beamont, the first Mayor, was to exercise an influence on the Council for almost 42 years, until his death on 6th June 1889. Had he survived three more days his death would have coincided with the 42nd anniversary of his mayoral installation. It is not without coincidence that Warrington Library and Museum were established in 1848, for these were among Beamont's many interests. The museum was formed by transferring to the Corporation the museum of Warrington's Natural History Society. The Warrington Circulating Library, a private institution and subscription library, was opened in 1760 and this was transferred to the Corporation, also in 1848, to be supported out of local rates. No other similar institution was so funded at that time, for it was two more years before the passing of the first Public Libraries Act, and so Warrington goes down in history as the first Borough to provide a Free Public Library.

In 1882 William Beamont, at the age of 84, and albeit not an elected Member of Council, was a co-opted member of the Museum, Library and Arts Committee, and its chairman. A minute in the Council proceedings of 3rd January 1882 also records his appointment to the Board of Governors of the new Liverpool University College. At a meeting of the Council on 31st October that year, a letter from him from his home at Orford Hall was read to the General Purposes Committee, reporting that he had attended the first Annual Meeting of the University College and, although established so recently, the college numbered 534 students and there was good promise of progress and success for the new college at Liverpool!

The first Council operated through eight committees: Water, Finance, Street Improvement and Lighting, Sewerage, Sanitary, Fire Engine, Market, General Purposes. One year later the Museum Committee was added, making a total of nine. This total had grown to 13 by 1882, a reflection of the broader sphere of responsibility which was undertaken by the Council in its improved organisation over the years. The number of committees has risen and fallen according to the responsibilities of the Council at the time. For example, when the

Council owned the Gas and Electricity Works there were Gas and Electricity committees, but these were lost with nationalisation. Despite many changes in the organisation of Local Government the committee structure is still the favoured way of operating, and this goes back to those early days of the 19th century.

William Beamont

ATTEMPT ON THE QUEEN'S LIFE

BOROUGH OF WARRINGTON
PROCEEDINGS OF THE COUNCIL
7th March 1882 (vol. 4 page 70)

It was moved by the Chairman, seconded by Mr Councillor Sutton, and resolved unanimously, that the following address to Her Majesty the Queen be approved and forwarded to the Mayor for presentation.

To the Queen's Most Excellent Majesty.

May it please your Majesty,

We, the Mayor, Aldermen, and Burgesses of the Borough of Warrington, in Council assembled, beg to approach your Majesty with our expressions of horror and indignation at the treasonable attempt made on Thursday last against your Majesty's sacred person, and our heartfelt congratulations on your Majesty's providential preservation from harm on that occasion. We desire humbly to assure your Majesty that we pray that by the blessing of Almighty God you may long be spared to be loved and honoured by your Majesty's loyal subjects. We avail ourselves of this opportunity of assuring your Majesty of our loyal and devoted attachment to your Majesty's throne and family.

Given under the Corporate Common Seal of the Borough of Warrington, the 7th day of March, in the year of our Lord 1882.

JOHN RD. PICKMERE,   WM. HY. BROOK,
MAYOR   TOWN CLERK

Reply received ...   WHITEHALL
                                               3rd April 1882

Sir,

... And I have it in command to assure you that Her Majesty is deeply sensible of the loyalty and affection of her faithful subjects.

CANON MORLEY STEVENSON
AND THE BEAUTIFUL WARRINGTON SOCIETY

H Wells

In City Beautiful all citizens, rich and poor, live together.
In one corner is the great City Church and the College and behind
each are gardens with flowers and shrubs and shady trees and seats
for all who like to sit and rest and meditate.

The City Beautiful, p6

One hundred years ago, the people of Warrington stood at the threshold of a new century, as we do today. The benefits and evils of the industrial expansion of the previous hundred years could be seen in retrospect and objectively analysed. Enormous progress had been made during the 19th century by figures such as William Beamont, in improving the town's housing, health provision and education, but much remained to be done.

The town centre was still surrounded by slums, the population had already outgrown its hospital provision and education was still largely in the hands of the churches. There were potentially destructive social divisions, while the new trade unions were developing a powerful counterbalance to the industrial might of the family-run manufacturing core of the town, although political control was still in the hands of a male property owning elite.

But, despite the heavy legacy of the past, the beginning of the new century was pervaded with optimism at the possibility of a new start. Providing the vision which they hoped might take the town forward were two prominent figures: idealistic politician Arthur Bennett and the liberal educationalist, Canon Morley Stevenson.

Canon Morley Stevenson

The Reverend Canon Morley Stevenson was educated in his native Brighton, at Windlesham House and Brighton College. He then went up to Oxford, where he graduated in 1873 and married Jessie Margaret Whalley, daughter of the Rector of Gaywood, Kings Lynn. Morley Stevenson began his career in the Church by serving as curate at Cowley and Great Marlow before becoming chaplain of Cetter College, Chichester, in 1879.

Only two years later he took up an appointment as assistant principal of Warrington Training College under the Reverend H C Stubbs. In 1884 he was made principal. He immediately set to work upgrading the college and, only three years later, on 1st July 1887, the foundation stone of a spacious new college chapel, costing £1,500, was being laid by the Dean of Chester. This is the only part of the former college to survive and now serves as a community centre.

Practising schools were then provided in Hamilton Street at a cost of £4,000. Fairfield Hall was purchased and converted into a hostel, and other space was rented at Orford Hall. When the Clergy Daughters' School left Warrington, their premises, which adjoined the college, were bought, providing a library, sitting room and art studio for students. The impressive hall was used for concerts and lectures by visiting professors.

Under the guidance of Morley Stevenson, the college, a Church of England teacher training establishment for young ladies, quickly gained a good reputation. At that time it claimed to be among the best equipped in the country. Yet, despite the large size of the premises, each year many applicants were rejected for lack of room.

Morley Stevenson was very popular with students and staff, whose interests he never forgot, and also with the people of the town. The values he sought to instil in the young ladies were derived from religious devotion and also from a wide, liberal education. According to the Bishop of Liverpool, who conducted his funeral service, Morley Stevenson's students were always encouraged to 'study liberally, think seriously and serve gladly.' He served the college for his entire career until his retirement in 1923, when he moved to

Liverpool and was appointed a residentiary canon of the cathedral. A kindly and approachable person, in his sermons he avoided pomposity, using simple lucid English. His speaking was characterized by 'perfect clarity of diction and felicity of expression.

Canon Stevenson, as principal of the training college and a leading figure in education, served on Warrington's Education Committee from its inception in 1903 until his retirement. He was a founder of the Warrington Pupil Teachers' Centre and the Municipal Secondary School in Palmyra Square. He served as Manager of the School of Art, Chairman of the School Management Committee, and Deputy Chairman and Chairman of the Education Committee. He also served on the Museum Committee.

Further to his valuable service on Council committees, Canon Stevenson was also involved with the town's social groups. He was chairman of the Beautiful Warrington Society, an active member of the Warrington Society and, being a great lover of music and poetry, was president of the town's Poetry Society.

A very popular man, on his retirement past and present college staff and students gave him a cheque for £250 (valued today at around £5,000) and an album inscribed with the names of over 800 subscribers. The Council gave him an illuminated address. His portrait in oils was presented to the training college.

Soon after his retirement in 1923, Canon Stevenson suffered a tremendous blow as the college he had served and developed was suddenly closed after a disastrous fire swept through the central wing of the building during the Christmas vacation. The Education Committee on which he had served for so many years strove to find alternative uses for the surviving buildings, but to no avail. Demolition soon followed. Happily, Morley Stevenson lived long enough to see its replacement begun at Childwall, although on a visit to see the work about six months before his death, he was injured, falling the entire length of an unfinished flight of steps. He died suffering from pneumonia and heart trouble on Monday 13th January 1930, at his home in Devonshire Road, Liverpool.

Works by Morley Stevenson

The Colour of Flowers, Warrington Literary & Philosophical Society Proceedings 1884-5

Recreation Evening Schools, Warrington Association for the Promotion of Technical Instruction, Warrington, 1888

Memory, a study in psychology, Warrington Literary & Philosophical Society, Proceedings 1898-9

Beautiful Warrington: What does it mean? Beautiful Warrington Society, Guardian Office, Warrington, 1906

The City Beautiful, Warrington Lit. & Phil. Soc. Proceedings 1906-7

The Idylls of the King, lessons on Christian doctrine and Christian practice, London, 1900

The Spiritual Teaching of the Holy Grail, six Lenten addresses, London, 1903

The Spiritual Teaching of Tennyson's 'In Memoriam', six Lenten addresses, London, 1904

The Spiritual Teaching of Longfellow, London, 1906

The Prayer Book Dictionary, editor

The Bible for Schools, editor

The Confederation of Church Schools, a paper read before the Conference of the Rural Deanery of Winwick, Guardian Press, Warrington, no date

The Education Question. A letter to the Right Reverend the Lord Bishop of Liverpool, SPCK, Liverpool, 1904

The Methods of Christ's Teaching, in Alpha and Omega, studies in the life of Christ, Church of England Sunday School Institution, London, c1910

Biographical Profile
Warrington Guardian Yearbook 1900, p 57

Obituary
Warrington Guardian, 18th January, 1930, p 11

The Beautiful Warrington Society

The Beautiful Warrington Society was founded in 1905 under the guidance and chairmanship of Canon Morley Stevenson. The first meeting was held at the Town Hall on 27th June and was addressed by Mrs Higgs, who had inaugurated a similar society in Oldham and was to visit Warrington again to offer help and advice in developing the nascent society. The initial meeting was followed in August by a circular giving information about the society, which was distributed to every household in the town — no mean task.

In order not to alienate the working classes, who might be reluctant to become involved with a movement promoted partly by the leaders of industry, it was emphasized that the society was intended to appeal to 'persons of all classes and opinions, and, as a consequence, a large and united band of workers will be brought together whose efforts will be directed to make Warrington beautiful.' The following year a determined effort was made to keep the interest of school children by distributing pot plants to them in Spring and judging their horticultural efforts in the Autumn.

In October 1906 Morley Stevenson wrote a 16-page, illustrated pamphlet explaining the aims of the society. Copies were offered for sale at ld and an additional 3,500 copies were distributed in 1908 to schools, to be used by class teachers as reading practice, then sent home for the parents to read. The pamphlet's opening paragraph was cleverly designed, first to silence the many cynics by forestalling their criticism, and secondly to inspire the necessary enthusiasm, optimism and determination to set the work in motion. The object of making Warrington a beautiful place might seem daunting but Morley Stevenson was determined to show that it was a practical undertaking, that work would not be in vain and every effort would, in the long-term, bear fruit.

The work of the Beautiful Warrington Society is to make Warrington a beautiful town. The members of the society believe that this is possible and they mean to do it. They know that there are difficulties, but they know also that difficulties can be overcome. They know that it will take time, and that many of them may not see their object accomplished; but they are content with the honour of starting the work, and they welcome the privilege of teaching their children to continue it. They are full of faith in the righteousness of their cause and of enthusiasm for carrying it out. They mean to make Warrington beautiful.

Beautiful Warrington, p 3

Several members of the Beautiful Warrington committee were also heavily involved in the town's foremost learned society, the Warrington Literary and Philosophical Society. Arthur Bennett was its president, so naturally Morley Stevenson was quickly invited to carry the Beautiful Warrington message across to that society. So, on 10th December 1906 he read a paper entitled *The City Beautiful*, in which he first set out his notion of the ideal city, then detailed the work of cleansing, beautifying and purifying existing towns such as Warrington, a task undertaken by the newly formed society.

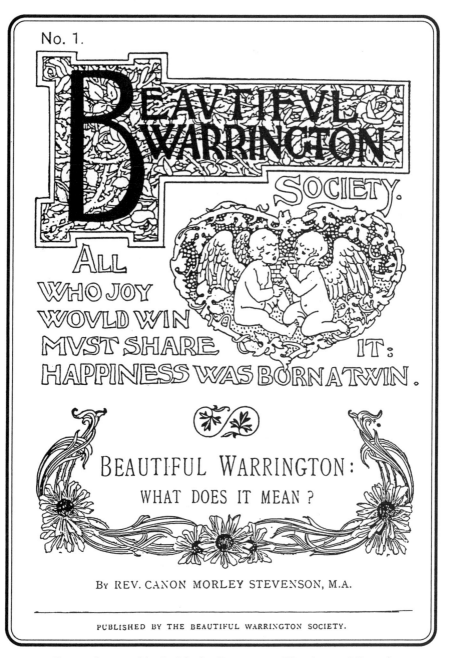

No. 1.

BEAUTIFVL WARRINGTON

SOCIETY.

ALL
WHO JOY
WOVLD WIN
MVST SHARE
IT:
HAPPINESS WAS BORN A TWIN.

BEAUTIFUL WARRINGTON:
WHAT DOES IT MEAN?

By REV. CANON MORLEY STEVENSON, M.A.

PUBLISHED BY THE BEAUTIFUL WARRINGTON SOCIETY.

Cover of a pamphlet by Morley Stevenson   (Warrington Library)

As well as the obvious need to improve living conditions in cities, with all that entails, Morley Stevenson is also careful to underline the importance of social cohesion and the value of public duty. Without this there can be no city, only chaos.

When in addition to the conception of a man's duty to himself and his family is added the conception of duty to his neighbour: when there arises a consciousness of his duty as a citizen ... then and not till then does the city spring into life. A city is a corporate body of which every citizen is a member. The interests of the city are the interests of its citizens. It should be the privilege no less than the duty of every citizen to think, work and live for the welfare of his city; to take a pleasure and a pride in helping to make it beautiful, healthful and good.

Warrington Lit. and Phil. Society, Proceedings 1906-7, p 6

The ideal city described by Morley Stevenson, with its wide avenues and handsome public buildings, is also a city devoid of social divisions. He is level-headed enough to recognize that inequalities of income will exist but the overriding impression is of social cohesion.

From the broad avenue run streets, alternating in width, broad and narrower, containing larger and smaller houses, for the more or less wealthy, for as I have said before, in this city there is not one quarter for the rich and another for the poor but all citizens live together. *Op cit, p 7*

The Beautiful Warrington Society had followed in particular the example of Oldham, but was part of a wider movement in industrial cities and towns around the country. In order to spread the message, Morley Stevenson helped to promote a national conference entitled *The Cult of the Beautiful in Industrial Centres*, first held in Manchester in 1906, when a Warrington committee member, Dr Markel, read a paper on smoke abatement. The following year another City Beautiful Conference was held in Liverpool, which heard papers on *Town and Suburban Planning* and *The Beautifying of our Cities*, again with the involvement of Morley Stevenson as Honorary Secretary.

Arthur Bennett was criticized by fellow councillors as an idealist, a utopian, but Morley Stevenson, at the same time as elucidating his ideal vision, takes pains to stress that although he is a social reformer he is also a realist, but that practical measures can and must be taken to improve the conditions in our towns and cities. The society's aim was to make Warrington a more agreeable place in which to live, by practical, realizable means, small scale as well as large. They promoted gardening, tree planting and the cultivation of flowers. They were also concerned with tidiness and the eradication of litter and graffiti. It was they who suggested, in 1906, that the Corporation should, as an experiment, put wire litter baskets in the streets, and that the tram car company should install receptacles for passengers' used tickets.

One of the aims of the society was to achieve significant smoke abatement in what, during the 19th century, had become a heavily polluted industrial town. That particular battle would not be won for another half-century.

They felt the environment could also be improved by tree and flower planting. Many of the trees in our streets, parks and churchyards were planted as a result of the society's efforts. The society's influence can still be seen in the Padgate Lane/Orford Road area, which was being developed at that time. The plane trees in Padgate Lane were provided by the Corporation and planted on a special Tree Day, 20th December 1907, and as the area between Padgate Lane and Gorsey Lane was developed on land owned by the society's president, Colonel Blackburne, a central recreation ground (Oakwood Avenue) was provided and the new streets were lined with a variety of trees.

Steel Street was planted with lime, sycamore, ash and plane trees. However, it was later found that, on reaching maturity, they were too large for close proximity to houses, and by the 1960s some had to be replaced with rowan. The streets around Oakwood Avenue are still pleasant tree-lined avenues, but more recently, in a retrograde step, the recreation ground has been divided up with ugly industrial fencing and most of the area closed to the public.

Beautiful Warrington Society Planting Schemes

... from annual reports of the Beautiful Warrington Society, 1906-10:

Hazel Street, trees and shrubs

Street near Fairfield Hall, trees and shrubs

Knutsford Road, trees and shrubs

Riverside and island, by Knutsford Road, trees

Arpley Station, trees

Bank Quay bridge, trees and shrubs

St Paul's churchyard, trees and shrubs

Crosfield Rec., Great Sankey, trees

Church Street, trees

Morley Street, trees

Training College drive, trees

Helsby Street, trees

Helsby Street corner, trees and shrubs

Egypt Street, trees

Padgate Lane, trees

As well as roadside tree planting, the society promoted the use of window boxes to bring colour into the drab, uniform streets. There are still some around, for example those on the Georgian council offices in Sankey Street, by Garven Place. To promote gardening, prizes were awarded in all the schools and, in 1907, the committee reported that 1,350 plants had been given to the 23 school departments visited. For adult interest an annual exhibition of flowers and plants was held at the Drill Hall or the Parr Hall with prize competitions in various categories. Outside exhibits were also encouraged and the judges visited nearly 50 gardens in 1907. At society events music was usually provided by T J Downs' band.

To publicise their aims and increase membership the society held open-air concerts in the poorer districts of town, such as School Brow and Silver Street, where 'free' musical entertainment was provided, but the audience then had to listen to a lecture about flower growing and making Warrington beautiful. Laudable as their aims were, there was an element of probably unintentional class superiority in their attempts to 'educate' the lower classes which, at times, may have caused resentment.

At the end of its first year the society had 335 members and 130 helpers, with another 2,500 junior members, recruited through the schools. Colonel Blackburne was made president and 30 or more leading figures of the town agreed to serve as vice presidents. The executive committee, under the chairmanship of Morley Stevenson, included such people as Captain Crosfield, Linnaeus Greening, members of the Council and other well-known residents of the town. The inspiration and drive came chiefly from Morley Stevenson and Alderman Arthur Bennett, while the organisation's success was largely due to the administrative ability and commitment of John Fairhurst, Hon. Secretary. The society continued to thrive in the period up to the 1st World War, but then more serious issues arose. However, The Beautiful Warrington Society, and others like it up and down the country, may have made a lasting difference to the appearance of our towns and to the attitudes of the inhabitants.

Warrington's Garden Suburbs

Not only concerned with improving the town itself, some members of the Society, including Morley Stevenson and Arthur Bennett, believed that, in order to take people out of a harmful urban environment, new suburbs should be built of the type promoted by the Garden City movement. As some members of the society opposed the scheme, either because they felt the society should only concern itself with matters inside the borough boundary, or for other reasons, a separate Garden City Company was formed to undertake construction of Warrington's Garden Suburbs in Grappenhall (on both sides of Knutsford Road south of the canal) and Great Sankey (in the triangle between Penketh Road and Liverpool Road). Residents taking up houses in the new suburbs were then given shares in the company, which still exists today.

The Future

The Beautiful Warrington Society was born in an era of great optimism which swept the country. It was the beginning of a new century, before the devastating and demoralizing effects of two World Wars and the Depression. Their task was begun but never finished. In the last quarter of the century the town faced new pressures. A sharp industrial decline took hold in the 1980s and continued, resulting in the disappearance of most large-scale manufacturing employers. A revolution in retail structure, with new out-of-town shopping centres, developed as the result of mass car ownership. The disappearance of churches, the creation of large new town estates, changing urban shape — all have had an effect on town centre districts. New political structures also took control away from the town. Pressure on public spending resulted in cuts in services, hitting maintenance of trees, verges and floral displays around town. None of this could have been envisaged at the century's start. Similarly, what the new century holds is a matter only for speculation.

Arthur Bennett, a councillor and benefactor, is still remembered in Warrington, but Morley Stevenson, who also achieved much during his lifetime, is all but forgotten. A recent issue of the Cheshire Archives and Local Studies newsletter published a photograph of him taken at Hale in 1908 and mistakenly interpreted what they took to be his 'pugnacious stance' as that of Winston Churchill, although the two men were a generation apart. (Newsletter 10, Spring 1997)

It is one of the aims of this article to bring the ideas and achievements of Morley Stevenson back from oblivion, perhaps to enlighten us at a time when we are again looking forward to a new era. The light of optimism, the quality of determination and the spirit of co-operation and public service shown by Morley Stevenson and the Beautiful Warrington Society may again light our way to the city of the future.

Beautiful Warrington Society Material in Warrington Library

Circular, 1905   Annual Reports, 1906-10

Annual Exhibition Programmes, 1906-10